INDEX

Joe Chamberlain had many qualities which marked him out as a commanding figure in an age of political giants. He was a notable municipal and colonial reformer, a supreme platform orator and, all round, a politician of great skill and independence. Such were his accomplishments. If his legacy in national politics is disappointingly meagre, it is perhaps because he ultimately lacked both the judgement and luck which might have helped him surmount the more difficult hurdles in his career.

Points to consider

1) Was Chamberlain a divisive, even destructive, force in British politics? Was he also a creative statesman?
2) What is the evidence in Chamberlain's career that he was a master of political organisation/electioneering?
3) What evidence is there of his skills as a modern professional politician and platform orator?
4) By his actions, he damaged the Liberal Party in 1886, and the Conservative Party twenty years later. What does this tell us about him as a man and as a party figure?
5) To what extent do you think that his personality mellowed over the years? Do you find him an attractive character?
6) Was Chamberlain too much of a provincial politician to be a success in national politics?
7) What were his positive services to a) the Liberal Party, and b) the Unionist cause?
8) Was Chamberlain in any way responsible for the eventual decline of the Liberal Party?
9) He was often characterised in his day as a juggler, a pedlar of assorted wares, and as an opportunist. Does he deserve to be defended against such charges?
10) Lord Salisbury cast doubt upon his judgement. What evidence is there that he lacked sound judgement at key points in his career?
11) A.J.P. Taylor's overall verdict was a harsh one; 'Chamberlain's great energies and great gifts were successful only in destruction . . . He was unscrupulous in his means . . . (He) brought a new bitterness into British politics. He was unsparing in victory and savage in defeat. Joseph Chamberlain was not a good advertisement for the imperial cause'. How would you seek to answer such an indictment?
12) Peter Fraser, a biographer of Chamberlain, has concluded that 'it is not his theories or policies but his style and method which have proved of most lasting significance'. Do you agree?

PERSONALITIES *and* POWERS

Hodder & Stoughton
LONDON SYDNEY AUCKLAND

Acknowledgments

The publishers would like to thank the following for their permission to reproduce copyright illustrations in this volume

The Mansell Collection, cover, p. 74, p. 119; Reproduced by permission of the Reference Library, Local Studies and History Department, Birmingham Public Libraries, p. 21, p. 24, p. 52, p. 55, p. 126.

From the author

I would like to thank the following people for their invaluable assistance;

Philip M. Walmsley, who carefully read the manuscript with the same critical eye once used to mark my sixth-form essays. His teaching inspired me with an interest in modern political developments.

My wife, Jill, who so patiently assisted in the preparation and checking of the manuscript.

British Library Cataloguing in Publication Data
Watts, Duncan
    Joseph Chamberlain and the Challenge of Radicalism
    I. Title
    941.081092

    ISBN 0-340-56316-8

First published 1992

© 1992 Duncan Watts

Typeset by Litho Link Ltd, Welshpool, Powys, Wales.
Printed in Great Britain for the educational publishing division of Hodder and Stoughton Ltd, Mill Road, Dunton Green, Sevenoaks, Kent by St Edmundsbury Press, Bury St Edmunds.

CONTENTS

INTRODUCTION

Joseph Chamberlain endeared himself to his followers and was often hated by his opponents. To Winston Churchill, he 'was the one who made the weather . . . the man the masses knew'. In Birmingham, they regarded him with affection; many of his colleagues were unable to share such a sentiment.

He was 'incomparably the most live, sparkling, insurgent, compulsive figure in British affairs' at the turn of the century. He had been primarily involved in the parochial concerns of his adopted town, but from 1880 to 1906 he was a major performer on the national stage, especially, after Gladstone's death, when he had no real rivals. The length of his career as well as the force of his personality ensured that he influenced and was affected by a whole range of controversial issues. Inevitably, he also came into contact with the other important statesmen of that era.

As his career developed, he was a player in moments of high drama, none more significant for the country and his personal fortunes than the events of 1886. In that year, he wrecked the Liberal Government by his opposition to Irish Home Rule, an action which was to be the watershed in his career. Having, in that epic struggle, dealt a devastating blow to the Liberal cause, twenty years later he was to do the same to the Conservatives by his advocacy of Tariff Reform. In such a stormy career, he inevitably made many enemies, arousing deep hostility and feelings of betrayal among his colleagues and opponents.

Chamberlain is an interesting and important person to study. His appearance made him a familiar figure on the political landscape, easily identified by his monocle and orchid. Yet if his picture is easily recognised, his personality is more difficult to unravel. Whether his formidable chilling exterior was a protective veneer or whether he was simply lacking in personal warmth is not easy to decide. However, if a full understanding of his character is difficult to achieve, the pursuit is worthwhile. Furthermore, the study of Chamberlain provides an insight into many aspects of life in Victorian and Edwardian England – political, economic and religious.

THE PARTY POLITICIAN

As a politician, he possessed so many talents that it may seem surprising that he never held any of the very highest offices of state. His tactical skill and fine platform oratory were allied to a driving desire to get things accomplished. Having decided on a particular course of action, he understood what was needed to get his policy implemented and could persuade the doubters of what had to be done. As a man of action, rather than a thinker or dreamer, it would be reasonable to expect that his long career would feature ample evidence of his achievements. At the local level there were many, in the national arena the results of his labours were disappointing.

Indeed, his significance lay less in any great constructive personal legacy than in what he represented. Democratic government in Great Britain is based on the party system and Chamberlain was the first truly modern professional politician. Whereas most statesmen of the era had other interests, for Chamberlain politics was his consuming passion. His private and public life revolved round the political world; as a female admirer who knew him well was to remark, with a mixture of admiration and frustration, 'the political creed is the whole man'.

His impact on party political life was enormous, not just on the fortunes of the two main parties but on the way in which both operated. He saw the opportunity presented by the 1867 Reform Act which had for the first time given the vote to the working men of the towns and cities. If their support was was to be won, new techniques of persuasion were necessary. Modern electioneering owes much to his inspiration and action. Modern techniques like mass meetings, doorstep canvassing, manifestoes and handbooks, and local and national organisation of political parties, were all part of his armoury.

His own political beliefs underwent a remarkable transformation during his career. He began as a Radical member of the Liberal Party. The Party represented a wide span of opinion, with the traditional, aristocratic element, the Whigs, to the right, and the more advanced, progressive

Liberals and Radicals on the left. In between were many members who tended to follow the leadership in whichever direction it wished to lead. Chamberlain diagnosed the nature of the party and his own role in it, in a comment in 1885:

> In the Liberal army, there must be pioneers to clear the way, and there must be men who watch the rear. Some may always be in advance; others may occasionally lag behind; but the only thing we have a right to demand is that no-one shall stand still, and that all should be willing to follow the main line of Liberal progress to which the whole party are committed. I do not conceal from you my own opinion that the pace will be a little faster in the future than it has been in the past.

The word Radical, (Latin, *radix* = root), implies someone who wants to get to the heart of the matter with a view to making fundamental changes in political, social and economic conditions. The Radicals of the early 19th century had been individualist in their approach, stressing that people should be free to act as they wished except when governmental regulation was necessary to remove some acknowledged evil. They were committed to efficiency in administration, and this involved modernising outdated procedures; they also wished to extend democracy by widening the suffrage and making improvements in the electoral system.

As the century progressed, they became more interested in using the power of the state to improve the quality of people's lives. The old ideas of individual enterprise gave way to a new belief in collectivism, which involved employing the power of the government to promote the well-being of its citizens. By such measures, especially after the extension of the suffrage in 1867, the new working class vote might be captured for the Liberal Party.

Into this world of the Radicalism of the 1860s came Joseph Chamberlain. As a successful businessman, he was typical of many Radicals who were often factory-owners and traders from the prosperous middle class. They had no time for the new and visionary ideas of Socialism which Marx and others were putting forward. They saw themselves as practical men, more down-to-earth, who looked for pragmatic solutions to social and economic problems. Nationalisation had little appeal to these private capitalists, but municipal enterprise was a different matter. Council ownership of essential public services could be an efficient way ahead.

Of course, by no means all employers were forward-looking or altruistic, but there were some local families who did have a genuine interest in the well-being of their employees. In fact, in Birmingham there was little of the class antagonism between management and workers so characteristic of Manchester and some of the other northern centres, though each group lived in very different areas of the town.

These employers brought to their politics a sound knowledge of the world of business management, and in many cases their attitudes were also shaped by their Nonconformist religious backgrounds.

THE CIVIC GOSPEL

In the mid 19th century, Birmingham was home to a number of distinguished and forceful preachers such as George Dawson at the Church of the Saviour, and Dr Robert Dale who preached at Carr's Lane. Such persons fitted well into Birmingham's tradition of religious dissent and political radicalism.

Among Nonconformists, Quakers and Unitarians were particularly significant, both groups strongly linking their beliefs to their practice in business and politics. Both were small sects, but in Birmingham they provided many of the city's Mayors between the 1840s and the turn of the century, as well as numerous other prominent figures in local administration.

The Unitarians rejected many of the Christian dogmas, including belief in the divinity of Christ, and showed independence in their moral judgements and actions. Their attitudes held an attraction for many influential people in Birmingham's business life. Families such as the Kenricks, Martineaus, Nettlefolds and Chamberlains were all dedicated Unitarians. They were aware of the town's social problems, and looked for ways of solving them.

Bad housing, poor working conditions, poverty, alcoholism and illiteracy were characteristic of most Victorian urban areas. Reformers sought an improvement in both the physical environment and the moral tone of their area. Such a sense of civic responsibility was not confined to the Unitarians and Quakers. Nonconformists of all denominations came to accept the 'civic gospel', the idea that it was desirable and necessary for the churches to be involved in local politics and for them to show a concern for the quality of life of ordinary people.

Thus politics was a Christian mission. As Dr Dale remarked of a Quaker friend and colleague of Chamberlain, he 'was trying to get the will of God done on earth as it is in Heaven just as much when he was fighting St Mary's Ward, just as much when he was speaking in the Town Council, as when he was teaching his Bible Class on the Sunday morning'. It was realised that only through political involvement and action could living and working conditions be improved, and the people to have a chance to live better and more wholesome lives.

BIRMINGHAM IN THE MID NINETEENTH CENTURY

As a businessman with a social conscience, Chamberlain found in Birmingham plenty of scope to indulge his reforming interest. It was a prosperous town, a commercial and industrial centre which exported goods all over the world. Those products ranged widely from steel pens to jewellery, from guns to brassware. Many of the factories were small units employing less than twenty workers, and conditions in them were often better than in much of the British factory system; it was not difficult for a skilled craftsman to establish his own workshop. Alongside such small-scale concerns, there were the larger foundries and industrial works. In a number of these, there was a tradition of paternalistic employers, who showed some regard for the quality of the lives of their workers, and this discouraged the vigorous trade union activity found elsewhere.

Politically, Birmingham was a progressive centre; denied any representation until the 1832 Reform Act, it had over the next few decades produced several dissenting politicians and reformers. It was the 'civic gospel' that provided the spur to their radical endeavours.

Yet if politically it was forward-looking, it was backward in its urban conditions and facilities. Many other towns, large and small, could offer a much cleaner and more sanitary environment. Though less overcrowded than Nottingham, and with less cellar accommodation than Manchester or Liverpool, it nevertheless had some appalling slums. As the central area was compact, the retailing, commercial and industrial areas were adjacent to the grim housing offered in the courts of The Minories, near Snow Hill, one of the most run-down districts in the country.

Fashionable residential areas such as Old Square and Colmore Row were very close to slums which, despite their proximity, were almost unknown to, and unvisited by, many better-off citizens. In congested courts which often opened at one end only, toilet facilities were inadequate, cesspools overflowed and rubbish accumulated around dilapidated buildings; sometimes, whole structures were in danger of tumbling down.

The road pattern was confused, with tiny, squalid streets adjoining each other at odd angles. They were narrow and totally unsuitable for the movement of either people or traffic. Whole areas were ill-lit, badly ventilated and had a pungent air. Not surprisingly, there were frequent outbreaks of typhoid and other diseases, and in these quarters the mortality rates were twice as bad as in desirable residential locations like Edgbaston or Harborne.

The basic problem was that Birmingham had grown so rapidly. From being a large market town in the 18th century, it had, in the industrial revolution, become a major manufacturing centre. Workers were attracted to the town by the prospect of employment and they came in droves; the population more than quadrupled between the census of 1801 and the mid-1860s, from 70,000 to almost 300,000.

Such rapid expansion required an adequate response from the local council, but this was largely missing until Chamberlain's reforms of the 1870s. Before the involvement of Chamberlain, many council meetings were held in a public house, the 'Old Woodman'; in 1874, he was to lay the corner-stone of a new Council House where more vigorous reforming plans were to be laid. He rightly claimed that under his leadership, the Town Council would 'go anywhere and do anything', just like the Duke of Wellington's army.

It was a fine building, more appropriate for a council whose conduct of affairs was at last going to be rejuvenated; soon, there was extensive development in the vicinity, and the area around the Town Hall took on its more modern appearance. It was in that magnificent edifice that Chamberlain had been inspired by some of John Bright's oratory, and it was to become the setting for some of his own most famous speeches.

The town whose administration he transformed in the 1870s was to be granted the status of a city in 1889; by then Chamberlain's own platform was no longer at the Town Hall, but in the chamber of the House of Commons.

IRELAND AND THE EVENTS OF 1886

After ten years at Westminster, 'Radical Joe', the rising hope of the Liberal Party, departed from his chosen path. The catalyst for change was the Irish Question, and its impact on Chamberlain, as on so many other 19th century politicians, was a dramatic one. The issue was no longer primarily religious, nor was it only economic. Gladstone had already attempted to resolve these problems by disestablishing the Protestant Church in Ireland, and by introducing the two Land Acts of 1870 and 1881. But these were palliatives which fell short of Irish expectations.

Though the question of land reform designed to create a class of more prosperous tenant-farmers was important, it did not tackle the fundamental problem which was the Irish people's wish to govern themselves. Home Rule was the solution of the Irish leader Parnell, though he implied that this might only be a stepping-stone to complete independence. As he stated in 1882,

> I wish to affirm the opinion which I have expressed ever since I first stood upon an Irish platform, that until we obtain for the majority of the people of this country the right of making their own laws, we shall never be able and we can never hope to see the laws in Ireland in accordance with the wishes of the people of Ireland.

The question of Home Rule was to prove a pivotal point in Chamberlain's career. He refused to go along with Gladstone who was converted to this policy, and after his break with the Liberal Party over this in 1886, he was increasingly to find himself on the other side of the political fence. He was on the road leading to office in a Conservative government but preferred the term 'Unionist' to describe his new political affiliation. For him, the issue of the union of Britain and Ireland was fundamental; as an Imperialist he would not be a party to the break-up of the United Kingdom.

A UNIONIST COLONIAL SECRETARY

The job that attracted him most was that of Colonial Secretary, for this would give him a chance to further Britain's Imperial destiny. By the time he had his opportunity, he was working in alliance with the Conservatives led by Lord Salisbury. The journey to the political right had not been an easy one, for the Toryism of the late 19th century had lost some of the

Disraelian interest in the 'condition of the people'. Chamberlain still was committed to social improvement, but was also attracted to imperial development and expansion.

When he became Colonial Secretary in 1895 the responsibility that confronted him was enormous. The British Empire covered more than a quarter of the earth's territory, and included nearly the same proportion of the world's population. There were eleven self-governing colonies with a European population of eleven million living in seven million square miles, plus an assortment of colonial dependencies with another forty million inhabitants. Yet the greatest British possession of all, the Indian Empire, was administered by its own department, the India Office, and not by the Colonial Secretary.

To Chamberlain, it was a 'national mission' for Britain to look after the affairs of this vast area, and he shared this sense of destiny with many fellow-Englishmen whose patriotism had been similarly fired. The Golden and Diamond Jubilees of 1887 and 1897 marked the high points of imperial enthusiasm. There was an air of optimism and confidence about the British nation, a mood expressed more loudly by the public at large than by its leaders. This wave of patriotic feeling was reflected in much of the literature of the time, as well as in many a popular tune. Sir John Seeley's *The Expansion of England* had done much to popularise the cause of Empire, and many people found it exhilarating to be at the heart of an Empire 'upon which the sun never sets'.

There were many motives for this new-found interest. The search for markets, a way out of economic problems of the 'Great Depression', an assertion of national (and even racial) superiority, and a moral belief that Britain had a duty to confer the blessings of civilisation on the world, were all features of this imperial sentiment. One aspect was an ideal of service and trusteeship combined with economic self-interest to arouse national pride. Lord Rosebery, the Liberal politician, neatly caught the mood, in his definition:

> I mean the greater pride in the Empire which is called Imperialism. Sane Imperialism, as distinguished from what I might call wild cat Imperialism, is nothing but this, a larger patriotism . . . the greatest secular agency for good the world has yet seen.

'Sane Imperialism' aimed to further the cause of the British Empire, but with due regard to the rights of native populations; it was seen as a moral duty, helping natives to advance whilst also doing Britain some good. The 'wildcat' variety stressed money and power, without any of the accompanying responsibilities.

Of course, not all contemporaries accepted the distinction. In his play *The Man of Destiny*, George Bernard Shaw noted how:

> every Englishman is born with a certain miraculous power that makes him master of the world. When he wants a thing, he never tells himself that he wants it. He waits patiently until there comes into his mind, no-one knows how, a burning conviction that it is his moral and religious duty to conquer those who possess the thing he wants. Then he becomes irresistible.

Imperial enthusiasm developed comparatively late in the 19th century. On the one hand, there were areas already colonised largely by British emigrants, such as Canada, Australia and New Zealand. These already had some degree of self-government. Separate Canadian colonies had federated into the Dominion of Canada in 1867, and the Australian colonies were also moving towards their own union (1901). On the other hand there were the new African possessions which Britain and other powers acquired by partition in the 1880s and 1890s. After the initial exploration of Africa earlier in the century, governments saw the potential of the region, and what *The Times* called a 'scramble for Africa' developed. After Britain annexed a new area, the next stage was left in the hands of private companies who settled the region in the course of their exploitation of its assets.

In South Africa, already divided between two British colonies (Cape Colony and Natal) and two Boer republics (the Orange Free State and the Transvaal), it was the British South Africa Company of Cecil Rhodes which was involved in the development of the region further north; the Company gained a Charter from Government in 1889. Rhodes had a vision of a vast British Empire in Africa, stretching from the Cape to Cairo, and wanted to surround the Boer republics which threatened his dream.

After the discovery of gold at Witwatersrand, many prospectors, mainly British, went to the Transvaal in search of their fortune. The arrival of these *Uitlanders* or outsiders in the Transvaal changed the character of this pastoral state in which the Boer settlers were predominantly farmers. The Boers feared both being outnumbered and encircled, and suspected the intentions of Rhodes and the British government. It was the lack of mutual understanding and respect between Briton and Boer which resulted in the outbreak of the Boer War in 1899.

TRADE AND TARIFFS

Chamberlain bore heavy responsibility during the Boer War, but when peace was signed his mood was conciliatory. He visited South Africa, keen to show that 'we have left the past behind'. While there, he developed his ideas on the need for a revision of Britain's trading arrangements. On his return, he could contain himself no longer. His campaign for tariff reform was his last great crusade.

Britain had been the 'workshop of the world' in the middle of the 19th century, when it had a virtual monopoly of manufacturing. A policy of free trade then seemed to be in its best interests. The more Britain could trade, the more prosperous it would become for such was its industrial lead that its manufactured goods would dominate the world's markets.

It was felt that national prosperity and free trade were closely linked, and the benefits seemed obvious to all. It was an American who was quoted as saying that 'free trade was a system devised by England to enable her to plunder the world'. The benefits remained as long as Britain enjoyed her manufacturing supremacy.

By 1881, a British economist, Edward Sullivan, was voicing doubts as to whether these advantages were still present;

> Thirty years ago, England had almost a monopoly of the manufacturing industries of the world; she produced everything in excess of her consumption, other nations comparatively nothing. The world was obliged to buy from her because it could not buy anywhere else. Well, that was thirty years ago; now, France and America and Belgium have got machinery, our machinery and our workmen and our capital, and they are sending us a yearly increasing surplus that is driving our own goods out of our own markets; and every year they are more completely closing their markets to our goods.

Britain's domination had been only a short-term one, and the combination of export markets lost abroad and domestic markets under threat from foreign imports made rethinking of its position inevitable. In particular, Germany restricted imports with high tariffs, and there were allegations that its products were being 'dumped' on the British domestic market at artificially low prices to ruin British industries.

In the so-called 'Great Depression' of the 1880s, Britain suffered a relative decline in manufacturing and trade. Its manufacturers began to wonder aloud if the traditional policy of free trade was still to their advantage, and producers in Birmingham became particularly alarmed. In 1881, a Fair Trade campaign was launched; it demanded retaliatory tariffs against those countries which sheltered behind their own tariff walls whilst eagerly exporting to Great Britain. The Prime Minister, Lord Salisbury, was sympathetic to the Fair Trade League, but the political costs of interfering with the orthodoxy of free trade were enough to cool his enthusiasm.

The difficulty was that to abandon or modify free trade would affect the cost of food. As a net importer of foodstuffs, especially wheat, any tariffs on overseas produce would raise prices. Thus Chamberlain in the 1880s, though not a complete free trader, was reluctant to support a cause which would result in higher bread prices and lead to social discontent.

By the turn of the century, the chances of a real improvement in Britain's trading position looked slim, and his outlook changed. His manufacturing constituents were not slow to point out the commercial disadvantages under which they laboured, and he saw in tariff revision the opportunity to bring about national recovery and bind the Empire more closely together.

His campaign failed, for the Liberals and the new Labour movement were able to emphasise the association of cheap bread, free trade and past British prosperity. For Joseph Chamberlain the Tory defeat in 1906 and his subsequent stroke marked the end of his effective career.

HIS PLACE IN HISTORY

His reputation was and remains a very controversial one. He was an active participant in so many struggles that he was bound to make political enemies, whether in the Town Council in Birmingham or in the House of Commons. His forthright personality, his 'pushiness', and his disloyalty to colleagues meant that there were inevitably more detractors than supporters.

Yet if he was loathed and reviled by his opponents, he was not without supporters, and in the country at large his popularity was considerable, especially in his home base of Birmingham. There were many admirers at Westminster, too, and Balfour's speech to mark his death was a genuine tribute to 'a great statesman, a great friend, a great orator and a great man'. Also on that occasion, the Prime Minister, Asquith, paid generous tribute to some of his qualities, and found him to be 'vivid, masterful, resolute, (and) tenacious'.

Since then, opinions have varied greatly, often according to the political leanings of the politician or writer. From such a lengthy and diverse career, most political traditions can find some things to approve of, but other aspects which they find distasteful. To the Left, the forthright Radical attitudes of his early days have an obvious appeal, though socialists might feel that some of his comments were mere rhetoric rather than genuine commitments to fundamental reform. His business instincts and his later Imperialist adventures would certainly make him suspect.

Liberals can extol his interest in social reform, and possibly regret that Gladstone never allowed it to express itself; if he had been given a freer hand to frame an active social programme, the rise of a separate Labour Party might have been at least delayed. However, it is Gladstone who is seen as the genuine Liberal, and Chamberlain's desertion of him to the enemy Tories is not easily forgiven.

For modern Conservatives, his early years are not easy to overlook; he scandalised polite society with his outbursts and it is hard to ignore his vehement anti-Toryism. However, by bringing to the party his reputation as a popular reformer, he was able to hand it an appealing policy of Imperialism and social reform. As such, he could be labelled as a Tory Democrat. The damaging gamble over Tariff Reform and his contribution to the electoral catastrophe of 1906 are a blot on his subsequent record.

Indeed, for all modern parties he is an uncomfortable figure to claim; like the curate's egg, his career was only 'good in parts'.

In the last years of his life, he was a confidant of J.L. Garvin, the editor of *The Observer*. Garvin's massive biography aimed to restore a reputation which had suffered from savage attacks. It is invaluable for information, and, written from an obviously favourable standpoint, it seeks to display the greatness of Chamberlain's personality and achievements.

It is the classic study of his life, though it dwells heavily on his career from the turn of the century; it was not, however, primarily a work of interpretation and assessment. Other studies have taken a different perspective. Of the more recent works, Fraser offers a political biography of his career after 1868, but neglects the Birmingham connection. He sees his real legacy as one of style and method, and does not dwell on his contribution to municipal reform.

Similarly, Richard Jay examines the career from 1868 though in a more critical vein. He sees Chamberlain as a politician with a clear insight into contemporary problems, but as one whose efforts were often marred by an inability to cooperate closely with others. Because of his personality he is viewed as a disruptive force in British politics, 'a misfit, unable to accommodate himself entirely to the main ideological forms in terms of which party debate proceeded, and incapable of operating successfully within the institutional structures available . . . inept in his handling of men and political tactics at important points in his life'.

Denis Judd's *Radical Joe* usefully covers the whole of his life though it does not offer much assessment of his historical significance. A much shorter biography is H. Browne's *Joseph Chamberlain, Radical and Imperialist*, which provides helpful background material against which Chamberlain's attitudes can be studied. It is, however, very selective in its coverage of a long political career.

Enoch Powell, writing from the perspective of a more recent practising right-wing politician, views his career differently. He sees 1886 as the key date in his career, the year which provides the clue to much of his previous and subsequent action. He is interested in the aspect of Chamberlain's revolt against established party thinking, on education in the early 1870s, on Home Rule in the 1880s and on tariff policy around the turn of the century. The insights are interesting for the writer himself, like Chamberlain, did not fit easily into the confines of one particular party; both men can be viewed as maverick personalities.

In this book, the intention is to provide a coverage of the main events in Chamberlain's life, but to place emphasis on those themes which are fundamental to a clear understanding of his ideas and work. His Radicalism, his involvement in the Irish Question, his imperialism, and his conversion to the cause of Tariff Reform are studied separately, as is his period as Mayor of Birmingham.* No real appreciation of the man can ignore the fact that he was 'Brummagem Joe' to the people of the Midlands, their political hero, and a name still held in high esteem today.

*Discussion of these key themes may be found in the Introduction, Chapters 2 and 4-8 and the Conclusion.

BACKGROUND AND EARLY CAREER

By birth and upbringing, Joseph Chamberlain was a Londoner. He grew up in a middle-class household, the eldest of nine children. His father, also Joseph, owned a wholesale boot and shoe business in Cheapside, and his mother, Caroline, also had a trading background. The family were comfortably off, living in the quiet suburb of Camberwell, south-east London, and were well-known as prominent Unitarians.

Joseph's religious background prevented him from attending a public school or going to Oxford or Cambridge. He was educated at small private establishments until, at the age of fourteen, he was sent to a progressive academy in Gower Street, the University College School. He was an able student who easily absorbed information in every subject, excelling in Mathematics and French. He might have been expected to proceed to University College, London, but instead he joined the family business when sixteen.

His father was unwilling to provide the funds for young Joseph to continue his study because he claimed that it would be unfair to offer an advantage to one child that he could not make available to them all. Such a lack of means seems rather surprising for he felt able to give £200 to any of the six sons should they decide to go into the Ministry. However, as a businessman preoccupied with profits, he was erring on the side of caution when it came to financing study at a university. Throughout his life, his son was to regret that he never benefited from such a start in life, and this lack of a higher education was a factor which later limited his acceptability in some social circles.

A BUSINESS CAREER

In 1854, at the age of eighteen, he moved to Birmingham to work in his uncle's screwmaking business. John Nettlefold wished to install new manufacturing equipment, based on an American technique, which would enable the company to produce superior screws more cheaply and at greater speed. To do so, he required financial backing. Joseph Chamberlain senior invested much-needed capital in the expanding enterprise. His son was sent to be the guardian of the investment, securing the family interest. It was an opportunity to gain valuable business and commercial experience in a city bustling with industrial activity, offering excellent scope for a young man wishing to establish himself.

The combination of Nettlefold and Chamberlain was to last for two decades, and it was a very successful one. Nettlefold, a knowledgeable mechanical engineer, was to prove himself an able factory organiser of the Smethwick works, whilst Chamberlain kept a tight control over the company's business transactions from its Broad Street headquarters.

Young Joseph was ambitious and committed to making a personal fortune, and his business acumen quickly developed. He was noted as industrious and methodical, bringing an obvious flair to the company's organisation and administration. He had a sharp eye for any opportunity to enhance the firm's prospects, and planned and executed many takeovers of other local workshops still using more laborious methods of production. The new process which Nettlefold had patented soon gave their enterprise an obvious advantage over their rivals, and as other concerns were swallowed up the partnership created a modern, large company employing many workers.

Not surprisingly, in this process they made enemies. There were suggestions that Chamberlain's energy and drive were accompanied by dubious practices, and that threats were made against anyone who held up a much-wanted acquisition. Predictably, these tended to come from those whose businesses had been taken over, and although good compensation was paid they resented being forced out of business.

LIFE IN BIRMINGHAM

In these early years in the Midlands, he was involved in local amateur dramatics, and was prominent in a local debating group, the Birmingham and Edgbaston Society, for which he eventually held all the major offices. The Society had a largely middle-class membership, and here he came into contact with other businessmen and well-known commercial and professional figures in the city.

In 1861, he married Harriet Kenrick, a member of a local Unitarian family, but she died in childbirth in 1863. He was later to marry her cousin, Florence, in 1868. The ill-fortune of the first marriage was to be repeated when, in 1875, she also died in similar circumstances. Meanwhile, his family had moved to Birmingham and become part of the large dissenting circle.

He was a Sunday School teacher in the Unitarian Church, first at the New Meeting House, then in Broad Street at the Church of the Messiah, a fine Gothic building constructed over the canal. He was made President of the Mutual Improvement Society, and taught at night school on leaving the office.

Not surprisingly, the rising Joseph Chamberlain, successful businessman and keen church-goer, was intent on fulfilling his social and political duties.

INTO LOCAL POLITICS

In the debating society, many of the topics discussed were political and Chamberlain's early attitudes revealed a sympathy for domestic improvement combined with a resolute stance in international affairs. He was always nationalistic in his outlook, and was no admirer of the 'peace at any price' foreign policy associated with Birmingham's new Radical MP, John Bright.

Within his own family, political discussions were commonplace and in private conversation he often talked about current issues. He even expressed the wish to enter 10 Downing Street!

Yet, preoccupied with building his business career and private fortune, it was not until 1865 that Chamberlain became actively involved in political life. He joined the new local Liberal Association at its birth in that year, and thereafter addressed local party meetings and campaigned for parliamentary reform. Demonstrations were held, and John Bright was a formidable and eloquent speaker in the cause. Chamberlain was impressed by his impassioned style and became caught up in the excitement of the struggle.

After the passing of the Second Reform Act in 1867, Birmingham's representation in the House of Commons increased from two to three seats and its electorate tripled, many of the new voters being better-off members of the working class. The Birmingham Liberal Association was to respond effectively to the opportunities now presented, and came to dominate local political life.

The increase in voters and the inclusion in the Act of the so-called 'Minorities Clause' required a more careful and co-ordinated approach by the political parties. The purpose of the clause was to give representation to the minority party in great urban centres, hence the third parliamentary seat. Each elector had two votes, and the Birmingham Liberals were keen to gain a broadly even distribution of the party vote in the hope of capturing all three vacancies.

Using the network of ward committees to canvass voters old and new, the Association ensured that, when the general election came in 1868, they were able to win all the seats with less than a thousand votes separating the Liberal victors. Joseph Chamberlain had a key role in organizing Liberal tactics, and the party's success was a considerable tactical achievement. Yet there were many critics of the 'vote-as-you're-told' committee, the party organisation which was soon dubbed the Liberal 'caucus'. The term, literally meaning 'a meeting of wire-pullers', smacked of American political methods, and had sinister overtones of corruption.

Even within his own party, there was some unease about the methods employed, but in other parts of the country Liberals were keen to take advice from Joseph Chamberlain and his associates. In Gladstone's words, the Birmingham Association had gained 'a kind of primacy' in these matters.

ON THE NATIONAL STAGE

He was much involved in the election campaign of 1868, chairing meetings as well as involving himself in questions of electoral tactics. He was by now an important figure on the local scene, and in November 1869 his active political career began when he was elected onto the local council for the city -centre ward of St Pauls.

Already, he was involved in the controversy over Gladstone's measure to disestablish the Irish Church. The bill ran into resistance from the House of Lords, and Chamberlain made his Town Hall debut at a public meeting to debate the issue. Such gatherings were often rowdy, and this one was no exception. Seconding the motion that the bill should become law, Chamberlain faced a noisy reception as each side cheered its own speakers and heckled opposing ones.

He used the opportunity to lambast the House of Lords, arguing that the Upper House had no right to reject a proposal that had been in the Liberal election programme and secured the approval of the Commons by a decisive majority. In a notably successful speech, he attacked the 'obstinacy or bigotry of one hundred or two hundred Peers'. The crowd warmed to his suggestion that these represented only the brains and talents of their ancestors, and (quoting Lord Bacon) that, therefore, like potatoes 'the best part was underground'. Though the meeting soon degenerated into the physical violence that often accompanied such occasions, Chamberlain's contribution to the meeting ensured that he maintained a high profile within the Liberal Party.

A much more sustained campaign was that for a national system of education.

Forster's Education Act of 1870

In the 1860s, English elementary education was in a backward condition, and various new organisations began to press for a major advance. In 1867, the Birmingham Education League was formed under the chairmanship of George Dixon, the Mayor, with Chamberlain as a founder member. Its purpose was to 'rouse the whole country to a sense of our present educational destitution', and to fight for a national system of elementary education, universal, compulsory, non-sectarian and free. To assist them in their cause, they launched an investigation into the state of education in their city. It revealed a lack of appropriate facilities, particularly for Nonconformists, the inability of many parents to pay for schooling, and the inadequacy of arrangements to enforce school attendance.

The League was efficiently organised, and it possessed sound financial backing. At the first meeting of the Provisional Committee, some £7000 was raised, with Chamberlain and his father each donating £1000 and father-in-law Kenrick giving a handsome £2500. For Chamberlain, the need for urgent action was clear; 'It is as much the duty of the state to see that they are educated as to see that they are fed'.

By 1869, the local pressure group had been transformed into a National Education League consisting of 113 branches. It was still based on Birmingham, and Chamberlain became its Chairman. In this role, he was to establish himself as a national figure, for when the Gladstone's government introduced its proposals, he was at the forefront of the attack.

The new measure, put forward by W.E. Forster, was designed to supplement rather than to replace the existing voluntary system. He was content to accept the voluntary provision that existed, but 'to fill up the gaps' he proposed that new non-sectarian Board Schools should be established. School Boards would examine the needs of their areas, and where educational provision was inadequate could build and manage new schools which would be financed from the rates.

The opposition was considerable, for the Nonconformists felt that Church of England Schools were being treated too favourably. They disliked the period of grace in which the religious societies could obtain grants to build more schools, for this enabled the National Society, a Church body, to launch into feverish activity to create many new ones. They also suspected that some Boards would use their funds to subsidise denominational schools. Clause 25 provided the scope for them to do so, for it allowed a School Board to pay for the education of 'necessitous' children; this provided an excuse for any Tories who wanted to support Anglican schools.

Though they won some concessions during the passage of the Bill, Chamberlain and his colleagues felt betrayed by the measure, believing that far from allowing the denominational schools to pass away, the proposals offered them the chance to renew their strength. He vigorously denounced the Bill, secure in the knowledge that there was much discontent with it among his Birmingham supporters.

In the course of its campaign, the League had a meeting with Forster and the Prime Minister, and for the first time Gladstone and Chamberlain came into direct contact. Gladstone gave little away in the encounter, but listened courteously whilst Chamberlain outlined the League's objections in an impressive and cogent summary. He was much impressed by the young businessman from the Midlands.

After the Bill became law in August 1870, the continuing educational battle moved away from the House of Commons to the local level where there were School Boards to elect. The Liberal 'caucus', normally so resourceful in fighting elections, received a setback in the first elections in 1870 and failed to mobilise all their voting strength. They still managed to win more votes than their opponents, but they had overstepped their resources by fielding too many candidates.

Chamberlain was one of only six Liberals elected, but he quickly became the foremost member of the Board. The Conservative-Anglican majority tried to use money from the rates to cover the fees of all the existing denominational schools, and Chamberlain fought their attempts tooth-and-nail in Board meetings, in a series of speeches and ultimately in the courts. He kept the issue at the forefront of his opposition to the Forster Act, for he favoured a secular system of education which left out all religious instruction. He saw Clause 25 as offering salvation to the Church schools.

He was also determined to reverse the result of the 1870 Board election. This time, he was in charge of party operations and he ensured that the party did not try to contest all 15 seats. Under his tactical guidance, the strengthened Liberal machine was able to gain control in 1873.

Other Issues

By the early 1870s, Chamberlain was known to the leadership of the Liberal Party, particularly because of his educational battle. However, an aspiring national politician needed a more all-embracing programme. He recognised this, saying that 'there is not force in the educational question to make it the sole fighting issue for our friends'. Ignorance was just one of the social evils, and in many towns it coincided with hunger and deprivation. He began to widen the basis of his appeal by taking up other grievances and weaving them together in a platform aimed at destroying the influence of the ruling classes. In a speech at the Temperance Hall, in February 1872, he claimed that:

> All class privileges have a tendency to herd together; you cannot tread on the foot of any vested interest but the corns of all the others begin to ache.

By such attacks, he won the widespread admiration of many Radicals and working-class Liberal supporters. His speeches in the coming months ranged over disestablishment of the Church, temperance reform, improved conditions and the vote for agricultural workers, and female suffrage. They established his credentials as a potential Radical leader.

He even briefly flirted with current republican notions. The reputation of the Queen was then at a low ebb, for, after the death of her beloved Prince Albert in 1861, there was resentment at the way in which she had retired into seclusion. The value of the Monarchy as an institution was in question, and he remarked to his friend Dilke that 'the Republic is coming, and at the rate we are moving it will come in our lifetime'. This was noted by his opponents, and became ammunition to be used against him in the future.

Disillusion with the Liberal Party

After his experience in the educational controversy, he became convinced that the Liberal Party was a 'gigantic sham', and in his speeches and writings he revealed his increasing disenchantment with the party leadership. He believed it to be a spent force after 1870, lacking in either principles or policy.

Such disillusion soon became outright hostility, and he began to talk of 'smashing up' the Liberal Party. In September 1873 he wrote his first article for the *Fortnightly Review*; it was a stinging rebuke, entitled 'The Liberal Party and its Leaders'. His comments reflected some of the disappointment felt by grass-roots Liberals in Birmingham, and the drift of his thinking was clear;

> If we are to have a temporary return to Tory practice, the Conservatives and not the Liberals are the people to carry it into effect. It is fatal to the sincerity and honesty of politicians that men should sit on the Treasury benches to do the bidding of a triumphant Opposition.

In November 1873, the Liberals followed up their School Board success by winning the municipal elections, and Chamberlain was chosen as Mayor. As his municipal responsibilities expanded and he prepared himself for a full-time career in public life, it was time to shed his business commitments. He had been a partner in the thriving Nettlefold and Chamberlain enterprise since 1869, and his resourcefulness in resolving labour problems and streamlining production techniques had played a major part in the growth of the company. In the process, he had personally become prosperous, and in 1874 he and his brothers sold their share in the firm. As a result, he acquired a fortune of £120,000, enough for him to pursue his political interests single-mindedly and entirely free from any financial worries.

timeline		
	1836	Born in London
	1854	Moved to Birmingham
	1865	Joined the Birmingham Liberal Association
	1870	Active in opposition to Education Act
	1873	Chosen as Mayor of Birmingham
	1874	Retired as a businessman

Points to consider

1) What was meant by the 'civic gospel', and why was it so important in the political life of Birmingham?
2) In what ways was Chamberlain's religion a spur to his political involvement and how did it influence his early policy attitudes?
3) Why was the Minorities Clause of the 1867 Reform Act so useful to the Birmingham Liberal Association?
4) Why did a Nonconformist such as Chamberlain object to the 1870 Education Act?
5) He was already a committed Radical by the late 1860s and early 1870s. Which of his policy attitudes illustrate his Radicalism?
6) What was his attitude to the Liberal Party and its composition in these early years?

2

THE DEVELOPMENT OF HIS PARLIAMENTARY CAREER. 1874–1906

part one: THE RADICAL PHASE, 1874–1886

At the age of 38, Joseph Chamberlain was a leading figure in Birmingham's municipal life. He was completely committed to his political career, and since 1873 had been Mayor of the town.* He had the opportunity to practise the kind of 'gas-and-water socialism' in which he believed, and many worthwhile changes were made. As a result, Birmingham provided a model of good government for other urban centres.

Chamberlain remained in that high office until 1876, though he already had ambitions to perform on the national stage. When Gladstone called a sudden election for January 1874, he cast around for a seat. There was no local opportunity, as the three Birmingham M.P.s were standing again. He looked elsewhere, and was selected in Sheffield as a representative of the Radical cause. There were four challengers for two seats, both previously held by the Liberals.

It was a brave move on Chamberlain's part, for he was an outsider, and therefore lacking in any of the trade union connections which would have been well-received in a city where the 'labour' question was highly significant. The campaign was lively, even riotous, and he was on the receiving end of several personal attacks. He was denounced as having been insensitive to the needs of his employees, as well as for republicanism and even atheism. Neither were the brickbats just verbal, for herrings and dead cats were thrown at him, one of the fish striking him on the head.

The result was also an unhappy experience, for though he polled creditably, he came third, and, therefore, failed to win a seat. He felt

* See Chapter 4 for a full discussion of this period of life.

wounded and affronted by his defeat, but busily engaged himself in his civic work in Birmingham.

He was still keen to become an MP for this would give him a more influential platform. He decided to abandon Sheffield, and began to search for some other seat to contest. An ideal opportunity arose in May 1876, when George Dixon decided to retire after some pressure from the local Chamberlain supporters. Almost forty, Chamberlain was returned unopposed, and he was able to retain his Birmingham constituency until his death.

As he began his parliamentary career, he had some misgivings. Though he might hope to achieve great things in national politics, he was losing the certainty of being able to implement his programme as he had been able to do in Birmingham. He wrote:

> What a fool I am to be willing to go to Parliament and give up the opportunity to influence the only constructive legislation in the country for the sake of tacking M.P. to my name. Upon my word, I think sometimes that both Birmingham and I will have cause to regret this step.

He had personal reasons for feeling uncertain and rather depressed at this time. His second wife had died the year before, and he had the responsibility for six motherless offspring. In addition, he was racked by gout, 'the statesman's disease', and perhaps physically exhausted after his bustling activity as civic leader.

An Opposition MP

At first, he was ill at ease in the House of Commons. MPs did not warm to his personality, for he was somewhat solemn in temperament, and very aggressive and outspoken. He showed no respect for accepted conventions, nor for more senior politicians. In the election campaign, he had savagely abused the Prime Minister, Disraeli, 'who flung at the British Parliament the first lie that entered his head', and this attack combined with his Radical* and republican reputation to make members wary of him. Many did not trust him, finding him personally self-seeking and politically dangerous. He was a threatening figure who posed almost as big a challenge to his own front bench as he did to the government.

* The Radical phase of his career (to 1886) is discussed more fully in Chapter 5.

Yet he made a good impression in his maiden speech of August 1876, on Lord Sandon's Bill concerning elementary education. He spoke for about twenty minutes, in a relaxed, conversational, style, and thereafter he was listened to with respect. He soon established himself as a backbencher with a future.

He objected to the lack of direction in the conduct of the Liberal Party's affairs, and became associated with a 'third force' in English politics. In this offshoot of the official party, he and his friends began to develop an alternative strategy. John Morley, from outside the House, and Chamberlain with his inside knowledge, began to comment on home and foreign affairs in the magazine which Morley edited, *The Fortnightly Review*. Sir Charles Wentworth Dilke was, from the beginning, another close political and personal friend.

Along with other Liberals, they condemned Disraeli's policy over the so-called 'Bulgarian Atrocities'. In May 1876 the Bulgars rebelled against their Turkish rulers, and the rising was put down with bloody severity. The Turks sent in their irregular troops, the 'Bashi-Bazouks', who carried out torture, rape and arson as they massacred 12,000 Christian people.

The Government was unwilling to condemn the slaughter. Disraeli at first tried to minimise the horrors as 'to a large extent inventions', and when their reality became only too apparent he seemed to condone them. He believed in putting British interests first, and thought that it was important to support Turkey in the face of Russian ambitions in the region. By contrast, Gladstone stressed the moral issue and became caught up in a great crusade against the iniquities of Turkish rule. The episode helped to rally Radical opinion behind him.

Having so savagely attacked Gladstone's leadership in the early 1870s, Chamberlain now recognised his value to the party. He didn't entirely share his moral outrage at the Bulgarian Atrocities, but saw the importance of the issue in rousing the country against Disraeli's premiership.

The revival of party fortunes encouraged Chamberlain to organise the National Liberal Federation, modelled on the Birmingham Liberal Association. According to Chamberlain, the new body represented the seven deadly sins; 'force, enthusiasm, zeal, activity, movement, popular will and the rule of the majority'. Its purpose was to give the Liberals an efficient political machine through which to organise the party for fighting elections and to mould and galvanise opinion in the constituencies.

Like the Birmingham Association, the NLF was soon referred to as the 'caucus' by its opponents. This was an attempt to smear the new body by implying that American methods of corruption and manipulation were being used. It was certainly American practice to put forward and publicise a programme and back it with a strong organization. Chamberlain admired this, and felt the Liberals needed something along these lines; it would help them develop into a more effective and disciplined force.

Chamberlain's objection to the Liberal Party had been to its state of drift. He believed that after 1874 the Liberal MPs were 'without a leader and without any policy . . . pledged to no measure, with no programme . . .'. He was anxious that the party should have a clear identity at Westminster and in the country. He hoped that through the caucus, he would be able to determine the path that Gladstone followed.

In Office, 1880-85

Gladstone had again taken over the leadership of the Liberal Party after the Liberal victory in the 1880 election. Reluctantly, despite Chamberlain's lack of any ministerial experience, he included him in his Cabinet, making him President of the Board of Trade. On balance, the Prime Minister probably felt it was safer to have him inside the Government where he could be contained, rather than on the backbenches where he might become a trenchant critic of Liberal policy.

At the Board of Trade, Chamberlain was able to get some modest changes onto the statute book. He took up the campaign for greater safety at sea, and introduced measures on Seamen's Wages and Grain Cargoes. His other reforms, concerning bankruptcy and patents, were useful, but he lacked the backing for a more constructive programme.

In Cabinet, he spoke and acted as the representative of the Radical element in the party. With his close ally, Dilke, he was keen to urge a more left-wing approach and made his views known on the whole range of the Government's work. His own preferred priorities were for land reform and the extension of the vote to agricultural workers. He was much involved in the controversy surrounding the Third Reform Bill in 1884, and led the assault on the Peers in the House of Lords who were holding up the passage of the measure.

His supporters were delighted that he did not mince his words. The young Lloyd George noted that Chamberlain was convinced 'that the aristocracy stands in the way of the development of the rights of man, and he says so

a note on . . .

VICTORIAN LIBERALISM

Nineteenth-century Liberals were deeply attached to the idea of political, civil and religious liberty. They were, to varying degrees, interested in progress, and had been supporters of Parliamentary reform in 1832. There was a strong tradition of religious dissent in the politics of protest; Nonconformists were strong in their support.

Gladstone joined the Whig-Liberal Government of Lord Palmerston in 1859. On matters of foreign policy, they shared a common sympathy for peoples struggling for freedom and self-government, though Palmerston's robust patriotism was not to his liking; on domestic policy, the Prime Minister was conservative in his approach, and wary of Gladstone's boldness.

When Gladstone became leader of the Liberals in 1868, he moulded the party in his own image, and his ascendancy held its diverse elements together.

The Gladstonian Liberal Party represented 3 broad strands of background and opinion:

1   The **Whig** element. The Whigs were well represented in the party leadership and in the Lords, less so in the Commons. Their outlook was well-portrayed by Lord Hartington;

> I admit that the Whigs are not the leaders in popular movements, but the Whigs have been able, as I think, to the great advantage of the country, to direct, and guide, and moderate those popular movements. They have formed a connecting link between the advanced party and those classes which, possessing power and influence, are naturally averse to change.

2   The **Radical** element. The Radicals, representing the commercial and manufacturing classes of the northern towns, disliked the complacency of such comments as the above, and were exasperated by the Whig approach to change. Labouchere wrote of 'the heavy lumbering coach of Whiggism', and Chamberlain illustrated Radical impatience in his remark;

> The business of the Radicals is to lead great popular movements, and if they are fortunate enough to stir the hearts of the people ... then ... the great Whig noble .. (will) direct and guide and moderate the movement he has done all in his power to prevent and discourage.

3   The **Peelite** element. These were the followers of Sir Robert Peel (deceased), who had split from the Conservative Party in 1846. Many had returned to the fold; others, including Gladstone came over to the Liberals. There were only 20 or so in the Commons, but some were well-known; cautiously forward-looking, they believed strongly in administrative efficiency.

The Whigs had serious doubts about Gladstone as leader, seeing him as unsafe, too bold and unpredictable, even though he gave them some of the main Cabinet posts. The Radicals viewed him with impatience, for on social questions he was too attached to contemporary ideas of individualism and laissez-faire. The Peelites admired his intellectual proficiency, and shared much of his outlook, especially on foreign policy, free trade and religion.

All Liberals shared the philosophy of Liberalism, but agreement on any programme of policies was less easy to reach; many Liberals had their own pet 'fads' or causes. Under Gladstone, however, the Liberals were broadly identified with:

administrative efficiency	the removal of (aristocratic) privileges
economy in government	self-help
*minimal state interference	caution in foreign affairs
free trade	anti-imperialism

*Radicals favoured a more active role for the state.

unflinchingly, though he be howled at as an ill-mannered demagogue by the whole kennelry of gorged Aristocracy and of their fawning minions'. The Queen certainly disliked the tone of his language, and urged her Prime Minister to rebuke his wild colleague.

In 1884-5, his differences with his colleagues became very apparent, and he toured the country offering an alternative agenda for the Liberals. The government fell in the summer of 1885, and this gave him the opportunity to put forward his personal manifesto for the next election, whenever it should come.

Some Liberals were shocked by the Unauthorised Programme (see p70), as it became known; amongst other things, he was advocating graduated income tax, free education, local government reform, and 'three acres and a cow' for agricultural labourers. However, it was the manner of his speech as much as its content which upset the Whig element in the party. He was not abashed, for he told an audience in Hull, in August 1885:

> I have been solemnly excommunicated by some of the great authorities who claim a monopoly of the orthodox Liberal faith . . .
> I am told if I pursue this course that I shall break up the Party . . .
> I do not believe it, but if it were true, I say that I care little.

Irish Problems

Irish affairs* loomed large in Gladstone's second administration, 1880-85. The agricultural depression of the late 1870s had added to the agrarian discontent, and his solution was to pass the Land Act of 1881. Chamberlain supported the measure, which conceded the '3 Fs' which the Irish had earlier campaigned for – Fair rents, Fixity of tenure and Free sale. Tenants were to be free from the threat of eviction if they paid the rent fixed by new tribunals. They were also given the right to sell their interest in the property, which in effect established the principle of dual ownership in land.

The Irish leader in the House of Commons, Charles Stewart Parnell, publicly opposed the Act, denouncing its failure to tackle the growing problem of peasant rent arrears. Parnell had successfully united the various strands of Irish opinion and created a disciplined party at Westminster over which he exerted great authority. His goal was a major recasting of the constitutional arrangements between England and Ireland; though not himself a committed separatist, he wanted Home Rule for Ireland, and nothing short of this would do. But to many Englishmen he was a dangerous rabble-rouser, responsible for encouraging or even coordinating peasant discontent in the countryside.

A stiff Coercion Act had accompanied the passage of the Land Act, but the pattern of discontent, unrest and violence in the countryside continued as before. Because of this, Parnell and other Irish leaders were imprisoned in Kilmainham gaol, though Gladstone had doubts about the wisdom of locking them up. Chamberlain was also more sympathetic to a policy of

---

* See Chapter 6 for Chamberlain's involvement in the Irish Question.

reform, though he reluctantly accepted the need for stern measures to stamp out disorder.

He was actively involved in negotiating the Kilmainham Treaty of 1882 which freed Parnell, and in the following years backed Gladstone in favouring redress of grievances rather than force as the better way of tackling the Irish Question. He believed that Ireland had a right to some form of local self-government, and in 1884 put the flesh on the bones of his ideas.

He favoured a Central Irish Board with powers over such things as land and education, and as his thinking evolved, the proposal was for a scheme of what he confusingly termed 'Home-Rule-All-Round'. This involved the creation of National Councils for England, Scotland, Wales and Ireland. He could agree to a substantial devolution of power to the Irish, but would not go as far as accepting Home Rule. He claimed that this involved recognising them as a separate nation, 'with the inherent rights of an independent community'.

Home Rule, and the Break with the Liberals

He was increasingly worried by Gladstone's attitude to Ireland, and his worst fears were confirmed when the 'Hawarden Kite' was flown in December 1885. This leak of Gladstone's commitment to Home Rule was designed to test the water, so that reactions could be judged. Chamberlain totally rejected the new policy, but when Gladstone formed a third administration in January 1886, he accepted office, and undertook to give 'an unprejudiced examination' to the proposals on Ireland.

When these proposals were made known to the Cabinet however, Chamberlain resigned. He was absolutely opposed to the idea of an Irish Parliament, the more so as there was to be no Irish representation in the House of Commons. Such representation, he claimed, would at least have clearly established the supremacy of Westminster over Irish affairs. He had other misgivings as well. The neglect of any special consideration for the rights of Ulster was a theme he took up, along with many other critics. He also disputed the terms of the Land Purchase scheme which was to accompany the Home Rule Bill. He was prepared to use any argument against a proposal he so disliked especially privately and among colleagues; publicly, he preferred to quibble over details, so that he would not get the blame for the confusion which would surround the Bill's defeat.

His genuine fear was that Home Rule was 'tantamount to a proposal for separation', a step on the road to the break-up of the United Kingdom. Yet the Bill was intended to do enough to satisfy Irish demands whilst maintaining the bonds between the two countries. The list of exclusions or 'reserved subjects' from the powers of the Irish Parliament was considerable; matters of war and peace, foreign and colonial relations, national defence, customs and excise, and coinage were all to be handled in London. The reality of Home Rule would have been far less than many critics feared.

Despite this, he was not to be placated. Alongside other dissident Liberals, including Whigs and Radicals, he attacked the First Home Rule Bill in the House of Commons. In a speech that won praise from many Conservatives, he helped to secure its defeat by 343 votes to 313. As he left the Chamber in triumph, Parnell bitterly observed; 'There goes the man who killed Home Rule'.

For years to come, Irish members were to see in Chamberlain another Judas. Some had never much liked him personally, nor had they much respect for his nonconformist religious background. Yet his past support for a more generous solution to the Irish Question had helped them overcome their doubts and cooperate with him. Their sense of betrayal after 1886 was therefore deeply felt.

That year was to be a watershed in his political career. His resignation and subsequent opposition to Home Rule had wrecked the government and seriously split the Liberal Party. In the following election, in June 1886, he was elected in addition to over seventy other 'Liberal Unionists', but victory went decisively to the Conservatives. Supported by this breakaway group, the Tories were to dominate the political scene for the next twenty years.

timeline		
1873-76	Mayor of Birmingham
1875	Death of second wife
1876	Entered House of Commons
1877	Launched National Liberal Federation
1880	Became President of Board of Trade
1885	Publicised his 'Unauthorised Programme'
1886	Opposed Gladstone's First Home Rule Bill

part two: THE UNIONIST PHASE, 1886-1906

Chamberlain was now in a very uncertain political situation. His main political aim was to defeat Home Rule. As long as it remained the Liberal message, any immediate reunion between him and the party was unlikely.

However, Gladstone was nearing 77 years of age, and if and when he passed from the scene, there would be a leadership vacancy in the Liberal Party. Some Liberals might then feel able to drop their commitment to Home Rule, and opt for Chamberlain and Radical reform. As an ambitious man, whatever his short-term problems, Chamberlain had reason to believe that over a longer period, his prospects were better.

For the moment, however, his position was difficult. He opened lines of communication with the Conservatives, and would do nothing to turn the Salisbury government out of office – as long as 'the Government which would take its place is committed to a separatist policy'. Though he was reluctant to vote with the Tories 'unless they are in danger', he hoped for a constructive partnership with the new Chancellor of the Exchequer, Lord Randolph Churchill.

Neither of the two men believed that coercion would solve Ireland's problems, and both wanted local government reform and improvements in the conditions of smallholders. But his hopes of any such alliance were soon dashed. Churchill was too bold for Salisbury and the Conservatives, and they were shocked by his reforming programme. His Cabinet colleagues refused to accept his Budget proposals, which involved lower income tax financed by cuts in expenditure on the armed forces. For Churchill, such opposition was the last straw, and he impulsively resigned in December 1886.

After this setback to his hopes, Chamberlain was keen to try and resume friendly relations with the Liberal Party, and proclaimed that as he and they were united on ninety-nine points 'three men sitting around a table' should be able to produce some sort of agreement. Held in early 1887, these 'Round Table' talks only served to show up more clearly the real differences between Chamberlain and the Gladstonians. Chamberlain realised that any reunion was impossible, and the talks fizzled out.

He continued to sit on the Liberal front bench, but there was no hope of any reconciliation as long as Gladstone remained leader. On the other hand, he risked losing his popular support if he became an ally of the Tories whom he had previously so vilified. Not surprisingly, he was depressed at the outlook in the summer of 1887.

An American Success

The Conservative prime minister, Lord Salisbury, came to the rescue by asking Chamberlain to go to the United States to lead a British delegation to

ELEVENTH Year. No. 558. THE DART. *Friday, July 8th, 1887.*

THE PARTY OF TWO.

J. CHAMBERLAIN :—Yes, we can get on splendidly. I will be Premier, and you Chancellor———

LORD RANDOLPH :—Oh! No, pardon me. You must be Chancellor of the Exchequer and I, of course, will be Prem———

(Left deciding it.)

arbitrate in a long-standing fishing dispute between the countries of North America. Between November 1887 and February 1888, his skilful conduct of negotiations led to the signing of a treaty between Canada and the United States.

He became very sympathetic to North Americans, and during his stay developed the theme of close cooperation between the English-speaking peoples. At Toronto, in December, he spoke of American citizens as 'our flesh and blood', and in the coming years he was to return to the topic. (By 1898, he had become pro-German also, and he explored the possibility 'of a new Triple Alliance between the Teutonic race and the two great branches of the Anglo-Saxon race').

On his return, he was well-received. The Queen, now more favourably disposed towards him, was impressed by what he had achieved. He declined her offer of a title, but was proud to receive her signed portrait, as well as honours for the staff who had served him during the negotiations.

He had another cause of happiness, for he arrived at Highbury to prepare his family and home for his third wife. During the social round of parties and banquets in America he had met the young Mary Endicott.

The Drift towards the Tory Party

After the abortive Round Table talks, Chamberlain's relations with the Liberals deteriorated markedly; many of his old Radical colleagues felt particularly let down, and were scathing about him. The Irish MPs shared their bitter feelings, seeing Chamberlain as the man who had frustrated their plans for Home Rule. Almost inevitably, he found himself moving away from his past and into a closer relationship with the Conservatives.

Many of his social contacts were with them. He had met Churchill frequently in 1885-6, and Balfour had often acted as a go-between in his efforts to sound out Salisbury. Other members of the traditional governing classes had come to accept him, for his manner was no longer that of the earnest Unitarian who had entered British politics two decades before. He had learnt to enjoy the material comforts and luxuries of life, and was attracted to the lavish hospitality and splendour of the great country houses.

Moreover, Chamberlain had always recognised that his old enemies could be persuaded to act on social questions in a way that the Gladstonian Liberal party could never be. Gladstone, preoccupied with Home Rule, was unwilling to allow the Liberals to adopt the constructive reforming policy

Chamberlain favoured. By contrast, he had found during his Mayoralty that Tory ministers could be helpful in assisting him with his municipal ventures. There was always the prospect that he might be able to achieve his aims through a Conservative government again. Indeed, he later remarked that 'in social questions, the Conservatives have always been more progressive than the Liberals'.

In other ways, his attitudes were shifting away from his early Radicalism. He was worried about the growth of Marxian Socialism, and saw that its influence was spreading in the trade union movement. He distrusted the activities of these New Radicals. He felt that they were a danger to society, because they brought militant ideas of class warfare and industrial strife into the political arena. Neither did he approve of their economic thinking, with its talk of the 'collective ownership of the means of production, distribution and exchange'.

On 'Bloody Sunday', in November 1887, a pitched battle took place between police and a crowd of protestors in Trafalgar Square. Two years later, the dockers won their demand for sixpence an hour after a month-long strike. These events highlighted the new atmosphere of unrest and the growing power of organised working men. Soon afterwards, the newly created London County Council, influenced by Sidney and Beatrice Webb, was developing an interest in new patterns of industrial socialism.

The ex-Radical Chamberlain also sharply disapproved of much of the Liberals' 'Newcastle Programme' of 1891. He saw its object as being 'to merge the individual into the state'. Items such as compulsory land purchase and universal suffrage were strongly opposed in his speeches.

By 1889, his sympathies had already advanced significantly towards the Conservative Party. His programme of reform was now of secondary importance to his desire to uphold the integrity of the United Kingdom.

Yet to retain his popular reputation and preserve his political base, he needed to demonstrate that a Salisbury-led Conservative administration could be persuaded to make useful concessions in the direction of social reform.

Conservative Reform

However, what the Administration also needed him for was as a pre-eminent figure with a national reputation. He had a touch of dash, and was an eloquent platform orator, just as Randolph Churchill had been earlier. He

Chamberlain was often depicted as a conjurer by contemporary cartoonists, and here he attempts to foist his past Radical programme on a reluctant Lord Salisbury.

could help attract the working-class vote and form a bridge between a Conservative government consisting largely of landowners and the popular appeal which had become so important in an age of a mass electorate.

Some useful measures of domestic improvement were passed, in particular, the County Councils Act of 1888 which pioneered a democratic scheme of local government for the counties. This was a cause which Chamberlain had championed since the 1870s. Other acts dealt with reform of agriculture in England and Wales, and provided free elementary education in all schools.

Some of these changes had been opposed by Chamberlain's former Liberal colleagues. He suggested other ideas that the Conservatives might take up, such as an eight-hour day for miners, shorter hours for shopkeepers and cheap train travel. Then, in 1891, he made his first public proposal for a contributory scheme of Old Age Pensions. The German Chancellor, Bismarck, had introduced such a policy two years earlier as part of a wider programme to improve the conditions of the workers and avert the dangers of social discontent.

The 1892 Election

By then, Chamberlain had travelled so far towards the political right that by 1891 he could share a platform with Salisbury at Birmingham Town Hall and propose a toast to the Unionist cause. The likelihood of his serving in a future Tory cabinet increased when, in that same year, he assumed the leadership of the Liberal Unionist group, on Hartington's succession to the family title and seat in the Lords. The two men had cooperated surprisingly well in the House of Commons since 1886, and both had offered broad support to the Salisbury Administration whilst reserving the right to vote against it on specific issues.

He did not neglect his Birmingham base. The local Liberals had at first tried to bury their differences over Home Rule, and work together on other issues. For a while this had proved possible, but by the late 1880s there was bitter feuding between some of the leading Liberal families – the Chamberlains and Kenricks on one side, the Cadburys on the other – and in the municipal elections of 1888 the two groups were in open contest.

Unable to count on the loyalty of the Birmingham Liberal Association any longer, he and his close associates established a Birmingham Liberal Unionist Association, and they succeeded in removing almost all of his supporters into the new organisation. At first, relations between the Liberal Unionists and the Conservatives were uneasy, for there were deep antagonisms which went back over many years. However, with an election looming, they drew much closer together with the Conservatives standing for seats in the Council chamber whilst the Liberal Unionists fought constituencies in the general election.

A New Liberal Government

The cause of Liberal Unionism gained a strong foothold in his home town, and in the 1892 election the new organisation carried all the Birmingham seats as well as performing strongly in several surrounding towns. The Liberals, with their Irish allies, won the election, and in the new Parliament Chamberlain continued to sit on their side of the House, but no longer in his old seat. However, prominently positioned on the third bench, he was well-placed to lead the attack on the second Home Rule Bill which was the main item in Gladstone's final administration. His assaults were notably effective, but this time the Bill passed through the House of Commons; defeat followed in the House of Lords where the Conservatives and their Liberal Unionist allies were strongly represented.

Gladstone wanted to move on to reform of the Second Chamber and had to be dissuaded by his colleagues. Somewhat ironically, it was Chamberlain, who had criticised the Lords with such verve and incisiveness a decade earlier, who in 1894 found himself defending its power to kill government proposals; Personally, the House of Lords seems to fulfil excellently the necessary duties of a second chamber. He even saw it as a bulwark against despotism, acting on behalf of the people.

Some months after the defeat of the Bill in the Lords, and after Gladstone's retirement, Chamberlain and his wife visited Hawarden to see his old leader and recent opponent. In their discussion, Gladstone made the unexpectedly warm observation; 'You have often been very kind to me'. Despite their mutual lack of understanding, there was, for all the antagonism, some respect in their relationship.

The Liberal Government fell in June 1895, and Salisbury took over as Prime Minister, with Chamberlain obtaining the job he had wanted since 1886, that of Colonial Secretary. Though a number of Conservatives still had doubts about his past record, he felt at ease with most of his new front-bench colleagues, both personally and politically. The defeat of Home Rule, the rise of socialism and the need to assert Britain's imperial responsibilities and opportunities all gave him a common cause with the Conservatives. Even so, he was convinced that the Liberal Unionists had to retain their distinct identity.

Meanwhile, his new position as Colonial Secretary* gave him the opportunity to develop his views on the merits of private investment in the colonies, a topic of which he had in recent years gained some salutary experience. The Governor of the Bahamas had convinced him that an enterprising capitalist could make a handsome profit from the cultivation of sisal in that region. Chamberlain sent his sons, Austen and Neville, across the Atlantic to assess the possibilities and the risks, and their verdict was an encouraging one.

In April 1891, Neville began establishing the plantation, buying up an estate on Andros, and organising local transport and labour requirements. He committed himself to the scheme, but despite his best efforts, the enterprise failed badly. Joseph Chamberlain visited the plantation in 1893, and was keen to provide any additional assistance that might be needed, but the hazards proved overwhelming. Crop failures, a serious fire, and a disastrous decline in the world price of sisal all ruined the prospects of the company which had to be abandoned a few years later.

For Joseph Chamberlain this was a personal setback. He lost £50,000, and was unlikely to find it easy to persuade other capitalists to invest in colonial developments. Neither was the Treasury likely to be generous after it had viewed the problems involved in such an initiative.

Salisbury's Third Administration

When the Conservatives won a landslide victory in 1895, Chamberlain stayed at the Colonial Office. The Prime Minister, Lord Salisbury, had a keen insight into human nature, and although he could see that Chamberlain was politically an asset he neither liked nor trusted him. He found him personally uncongenial and his views distasteful. Social relations between Highbury, the Chamberlain home, and his own at Hatfield House were firmly established, but he was not relaxed in his company. He could recognise Chamberlain's drive and resolution, but he found him cold and ambitious; he also suspected that he lacked judgement and he was too inexperienced in overseas matters.

---

* See Chapter 7 for his work on behalf of the British Empire.

a note on . . .

THE POLITICAL RIGHT IN LATE-VICTORIAN AND EDWARDIAN TIMES

Conservative Prime Ministers
Lord Salisbury   1885
1886-92
1895-1902

Arthur Balfour   1902-05

Liberal Unionist Support
After the Home Rule split in 1886, Chamberlain (then a Radical) and Hartington (a Whig) left the Liberal Party, and took some of their supporters with them as Liberal Unionists.

In the 1886-92 government, the 79 Liberal Unionists generally backed the Conservatives, especially over Ireland.

Between 1895-1902, the 50 Liberal Unionists supported the Conservatives, and pursued an agreed set of policies. Chamberlain and others served in this Conservative and Liberal Unionist government, as they initially did in the Balfour that government that followed.

The Term 'Unionism'
The Liberal Unionists were a separate organisation from the Conservatives. They were allies, and although the political and social links were to become ever closer, they did not merge, and become the Conservative and Unionist Party until shortly before World War One.

Chamberlain liked to call himself a Unionist after 1895, and the Conservatives increasingly adopted the name to describe themselves. The term Unionist gradually fell into disuse soon after World War One, though it remains as part of the official title today, the Conservative and Unionist Party.

NB. Many Examiners regularly use the term Unionist when writing of the Salisbury and Balfour Administrations.

Salisbury warned his colleagues of his fears, but his views were ignored and he contented himself with asides to those who knew him well. Some were amusing as well as dismissive. In *My Autobiography*, Margot Asquith recalled one of his remarks:

> I heard (Chamberlain) at Grosvenor House. Let me see . . . what was he speaking about? . . . (reflectively) Australian washerwomen . . . or some such thing.

Lady Balfour remarked, in November 1895, that she 'never heard (Salisbury) talk of any colleague as he does of him, says Chamberlain wants to go to war with every Power in the world, and has no thought but Imperialism'.

Chamberlain had little respect for Salisbury either. He neither admired him nor did he care for his political approach. He could respect Gladstone's massive authority and his prodigious energy, but found no similar qualities in Salisbury. However, he held the job he wanted, and now had the chance to show his commitment to Britain's Imperial destiny. The affairs of the Empire aroused his full attention and interest, and his patriotic rhetoric found favour with the British people who were in a jingoistic mood.

As Colonial Secretary, he introduced the bill which brought about the establishment of the Commonwealth of Australia. He was also interested in the 'underdeveloped estates of the realm', and observed that the landlord of a great estate would spend some of his money on improving his property. However, he found it difficult to get money out of the Treasury, and this limited his success as a colonial reformer.

Events in South Africa

Chamberlain soon became deeply involved in events in South Africa. In 1886, gold was discovered on the Witwatersrand in the independent republic of Transvaal; a flood of 'Uitlanders' or outsiders poured in, many of them British. They were unwelcome to many of the Boers who were keen to protect their own traditional way of life. The administration of President Kruger denied the newcomers the civil rights that Boers received, though it placed a heavy burden of taxation upon them.

Relations between the two communities deteriorated, and the Prime Minister of Cape Colony, Cecil Rhodes, saw the opportunity of using the Uitlanders' discontent as a means of overthrowing the Kruger regime. Rhodes was an enthusiast for Empire development and expansion, and

British control of the Transvaal would enable him to fulfil his dream of building a Cape-to-Cairo railway running entirely through British territory.

He arranged for some of the Uitlanders to organise a rebellion inside the Transvaal, and this gave him the excuse for sending in an invading force under his friend and employee, Dr Starr Jameson, to 'protect' British interests. The rising in December 1895 never got under way, but Jameson's band of horsemen still rode in. The Jameson Raid was a total failure, and was soon put down.

In Britain, there was much interest in the role of the Colonial Office and in Chamberlain's conduct of affairs. There was plenty of ammunition for his opponents who accused him of complicity in the Raid. Though a Select Committee of the House of Commons cleared him of any responsibility, historians have generally been less lenient. Whilst he did not conceive of the plan, at the very least he knew of its existence and was content to let it proceed.

The Boer War, 1899-1902

In the years leading up to the war of 1899-1902, Chamberlain's stance was generally anti-Boer. He sympathised with the position of the Uitlanders, but was even more interested the extension of British influence in South Africa. The Transvaal was a wealthy part of the region, and likely to be of great importance in the future. Kruger's Government was an obstacle to his ambitions.

He hoped to resolve the Uitlander problem without the need for any hostilities. After the appointment of Sir Alfred Milner as High Commissioner for South Africa, this became less likely, for Milner soon came to the conclusion that war was almost inevitable. As a momentum for war developed, it was easy for critics to portray Chamberlain as an Imperialist adventurer who played for dangerously high stakes. His involvement only served to confirm Lord Salisbury's pessimism and alarm.

Conferences between British and Boer leaders took place, but neither side felt able to make sufficient compromises to settle the dispute. Kruger was aggressive and obstinate; British public opinion had been prepared for a war on behalf of the Uitlanders. Neither side would wait indefinitely, and war began in 1899.

Initially, the Boers were successful and gained several victories. British garrisons were besieged in Ladysmith, Kimberley and Mafeking, and it was not until large reinforcements were sent from Britain, with backing from Australia, New Zealand and Canada, that the tide turned in Britain's favour. Mafeking was relieved in May 1900, having been under siege for 217 days, and by September the last Boer army in the field had been defeated. Even then, the Boers fought on in guerilla style, their soldiers sustained by the support of farmers on the veldt. It was not until May 1902 that the Treaty of Vereeniging brought the fighting to an end; the Transvaal and Orange Free State became British colonies.

Altogether, 5,744 British troops had been killed, over 20,000 wounded, and another 16,000 died from disease. Boer deaths are unknown, though estimates of the number killed in the fighting are usually in the region of 4,000. Apart from the tragic loss of life, Britain also suffered a loss of reputation. It had shocked many people that the army had needed to resort to 'methods of barbarism' to defeat the Boers, for in the last two years British soldiers had burned down Boer homesteads, and moved civilians into so-called 'concentration camps'. Many thousands of them died because of undernourishment and as a result of poor hygiene and sanitation.

When the war was over, Chamberlain recognised the need not only for reconstruction, but also for reconciliation, and he set off for South Africa. In Pretoria, he announced that 'Henceforth, we are one nation under one flag. We have left the past behind'.

Tariffs and Defeat

A few months before this visit, Lord Salisbury had resigned as Prime Minister. Balfour's succession was generally anticipated, though Chamberlain may have still had some hopes of assuming the premiership. He was still a lively and popular figure on the political scene, with many supporters who were keen to see him in Downing Street. One sympathetic magazine described him as 'no ephemeron, no mere man of the hour. He is the man of tomorrow, and the day after tomorrow'.

Chamberlain did not push his claim in the months before Salisbury's retirement, for he was a realist who understood that the Conservative Party would want one of its own members to lead it; after all, he was still a Liberal Unionist, a member of a group with its own distinctive identity. He also felt some loyalty to Balfour who had smoothed his relations with the Conservatives in the years after 1886, and was willing to serve under him if he could still have an influential role. He remained as Colonial Secretary.

On his return from South Africa, he launched his last campaign. Still committed to the idea of Empire, he produced a plan for Imperial Preference to help bind the colonies closer to Britain. This involved a major revision of British trading policy,* as Britain had long been wedded to the doctrine of Free Trade. Chamberlain saw this policy as obsolete, and wanted to impose tariffs on goods from outside the Empire, with no or lower duties on those from within it. As other countries constructed tariff walls, retaliatory measures were needed by Britain if manufacturers were to protect themselves.

With disagreements in the Balfour Government over the issue, Chamberlain resigned his Cabinet post and took his campaign to the country. He was unable to rally opinion behind him, for the association of cheap bread and free trade was a strong one in people's minds. Balfour rightly saw that:

> the prejudice against a small tax on food is not the fad of a few imperfectly informed theorists, it is a deep-rooted prejudice affecting a large mass of voters, especially the poorest class, which it will be a matter of extreme difficulty to overcome.

Chamberlain's attempt to convert the party only served to expose its divisions on the matter, and when the election came in 1906 such disunity was a factor in the massive Unionist defeat. By following his convictions and pushing so hard to see them put into effect, he had brought about another rift; as he had split the Liberals in 1886, so he did the same for their opponents twenty years later.

His effective political career was at an end. Shortly after the election he suffered a stroke which rendered him 'a muted cripple', although his death did not occur until eight years later, in 1914.

timeline		
	1887	'Round Table' talks failed
	1888	Third marriage (aged 52)
	1889	Declared himself to be a 'Unionist'
	1895 June	Became Colonial Secretary
	Dec	Jameson Raid
	1899	Boer War began
	1902 May	War ended
	July	At Colonial Office, under Balfour as PM

---

* See Chapter 8 for details of the Tariff Reform campaign.

1903 May	Major speech; advocated Tariff Reform
Sept	Resigned from Balfour Government
1903-06	Campaigned for Tariff Reform
1906	Crushing election defeat for the Balfour Government

part three: HIS DEVELOPING IDEAS, 1876-1906

Throughout his career, although Chamberlain held his views very firmly, they were by no means always the same ones. It was a regular taunt made by his opponents that he lacked principle and was opportunistic, changing his opinions when this seemed to his advantage. Politicians and journalists, writers and cartoonists of the day noted these alleged qualities and frequently exploited them. Because he was ambitious and changed his mind on important issues, he was an obvious target, and the attacks on him ranged from the relatively mild to the savage. Lloyd George was able to get a good laugh in Chamberlain's home town with his comparison of 'Joe to the political contortionist at the Pavilion'.

To have held different opinions, even strong ones, is not surprising. His career was a remarkable one, and in its long duration, he confronted some great issues ranging from education to Home Rule, from the treatment of the Uitlanders to Britain's future trading policy. It would have been amazing if in thirty years as an MP he was entirely consistent.

Inconsistency might have been better understood if his party allegiance had remained constant. In his case, however, the changes seem more fundamental, for they involved a total change of stance, from an aggressive Radical position to a defensive Unionist one. The man who was denounced as a wild agitator and socialist was himself later to brand the progressive element in the Liberal Party as 'Radicals'. When he was a Radical, he held Radical ideas fervently; when he was a Unionist, his approach was markedly more sympathetic to that of the Conservatives. The shift did not trouble him, and he never claimed to have always held the same outlook; indeed, he believed that to have done so would have been a sign of political immaturity.

The Radical Period

Ultimately, the party mattered less than the cause he was currently pursuing. When he entered the House of Commons in 1876, he was an impatient Radical, frustrated not just by the Conservatives but also by the aristocratic Whigs in his own party; he believed that they did Tory work in a Liberal uniform.

As a committed Radical, he was concerned to spotlight social injustice and tackle its causes. The highlight of his career in this phase was probably the period 1884-5 when he was involved in the dispute with the House of Lords and went on to develop a wide-ranging manifesto, the Unauthorised Programme.

In his tour to publicise his ideas, he roused his audiences by suggesting far-reaching changes, ranging from free primary education to full local government for the counties, from land reform to grant the labourer a stake in the soil to manhood suffrage:

> I do not want you to think that I suggest to you that legislation can accomplish all that we desire, and, above all, I would not lead you into wild and revolutionary projects which would upset unnecessarily the existing order of things. But, on the other hand, I want you not to accept as final or as perfect, arrangements under which hundreds of thousands, nay millions, of your fellow-countrymen are subjected to untold privations and misery, with the evidence all around them of accumulated wealth and unbounded luxury.

To every Tory and to the majority of the aristocracy, his programme seemed very alarming, though what seemed so then was to become the commonplace of the future. It wasn't just the policies that worried them, it was the inflammatory mode of expression. To the landowners, he was a dangerous agitator, and they were outraged by his idea that they should pay a 'ransom' to secure their privileged position.

It seemed all the more menacing because to some of them there was the smell of socialism about his ideas. The term was loosely used, and few people had any real idea of what it meant (see A Note on Socialism overleaf). To attack him for his socialism was just a way of expressing horror at his language and proposals, just as it was when he was denounced as a communist or an anarchist. If socialism aimed at replacing capitalism by some scheme of public ownership or nationalisation, he was against it; he was similarly opposed to any idea of equality. But wanted to:

> remove inequalities which now, in my opinion, rest unjustly upon the mass of the necessitous classes . . . I do not believe that

a note on . . .

SOCIALISM

The word Socialism was used loosely in late-Victorian England. It was often employed by more conservative politicians to describe anyone who was more radical than they themselves were; e.g., Gladstone spoke of unflatteringly of Chamberlain as being a socialist in the mid-1880s. Like many others, he feared the advance of such a doctrine.

Chamberlain himself used the term to describe his own attitudes, and to describe some contemporary policies. He even claimed that the Forster Education Act was 'socialist', and went on to say that 'every kindly act of legislation' fell into this category. He maintained that socialism was all about social policies designed to improve the lot of the ordinary person.

Used in this way, the word was in common currency. In the broadest sense, a socialist was any person who was prepared to use the power of the state to benefit the mass of people; varying degrees, such a socialist would accept government intervention to modify the capitalist system. Sir William Harcourt, the Liberal MP, is credited with the remark: 'We are all socialists now' (1887).

But Harcourt was certainly not saying that there were many late-Victorians who had been converted to the creed of Karl Marx or other writers!

The word was often used in local government in connection with the provision of gas, water or housing; municipal trading (like Chamberlain's municipalisation of the gas and water supply) was often referred to as 'municipal Socialism'. Chamberlain said that he was 'enough of a socialist to believe that services which by their nature, best function as monopolies, should be under public control'. Again, such policies had nothing to do with Marxist ideology.

There were very few people in the late nineteenth century who could be described as socialists by any modern definition, perhaps a few thousand who belonged to various avowedly socialist societies. Some of these societies were Marxist, as was the Social Democratic Federation of Henry Hyndman.

Politicians such as Chamberlain had no time for such creeds, for they believed that these 'New Radicals', as he called them, were motivated by the politics of envy, class hatred and industrial strife; he had no time for anyone who was agitating for the overthrow of capitalism. Successful businessman that he was, he strongly believed in the virtues of hard work, effort and enterprise.

there can ever be an absolute equality of conditions, and I think that nothing would be more undesirable than that we should remove the stimulus to industry and thrift and exertion . . . I am opposed to confiscation in every shape and form.

Though his speeches provoked attacks from some quarters, he had the compensation that he was, in Garvin's words, 'the idol of millions, and the delight of the friends whose highest hopes he had far exceeded'. Many tributes were paid to him, and the young Ramsay MacDonald noted that the Scots were inspired and felt themselves 'captained and marching' after hearing him speak; they liked the earnest candour of the man, and his 'bold audacity struck the imagination of the country'.

The Unionist Period

The controversy over Home Rule diverted him from this Radical path, and gradually he became more identified with his erstwhile opponents, sometimes defending ideas and institutions he had previously attacked. Having at one time anticipated the likely dawning of a republic, he became a truly patriotic Unionist, concerned to see the Monarchy placed at the heart of the Empire. The Peers, once the target for so much of his ridicule, were now seen as fulfilling a crucial role; no longer were they seen as 'irresponsible without independence, obstinate without courage, arbitrary without judgement and arrogant without knowledge'. By the time of the Constitutional Crisis of 1909-11, he felt that the 'Lords was justified in holding up measures for which the government had no popular mandate', a claim that Lord Salisbury had ventured to put forward in 1884-5. He strongly resisted the Parliament Bill in his declining years, and echoed the view that the second chamber was the only bulwark against socialism and destruction. Earlier in his career, he had doubted if it had any role at all.

Inconsistency?

Chamberlain's apologists point to an underlying consistency in his career. His biographer and friend, J.L. Garvin, even tried to assert this claim in relation to the House of Lords, questioning the view that he moved from being a fierce critic to a staunch defender of that institution. He felt that Chamberlain's attitude changed 'in proportion to an immense change in public circumstances'. In earlier confrontations, such as the dispute over the Third Reform Bill, the Lords had been out of step with public opinion; ten years later, he felt that the House of Commons was out of step on Home Rule, for the government was pressing a measure unwanted by the people. Certainly, the electorate showed no enthusiasm in voting for a Liberal Party committed to Home Rule, though it is difficult to prove that, outside Ulster, the issue was an obvious vote-loser.

Chamberlain concluded that any government with a majority in the House of Commons might be able to pass radical, even dangerous, legislation such as Home Rule, unless there was a second chamber to allow an opportunity for reconsideration. He therefore wanted some form of barrier against precipitate change. On the other hand, he always felt that the hereditary system was a ridiculous way of choosing the members of that assembly, and would have preferred an elected chamber. In the Parliament Bill, the Liberals were intent on reducing its powers, whilst maintaining the basis of its composition.

Garvin also claimed that there was one consistent theme which survived Chamberlain's changing allegiance, and this was his concern for the social question; as he expressed it in 1885, it was: 'How to promote the greater happiness of the mass of the people, how to increase their enjoyment of life – that is the problem of the future'. Although his social conscience was more evident in his early years, his later speeches, often on different subjects, showed he remained interested in seeing his social plans achieved.

He was never a do-nothing Tory in the Salisbury mould. In public, he praised the Salisbury Government of 1886-92 for any concessions to the progressive viewpoint, but in private he badgered and prodded its members to go further. He later urged the introduction of Old Age Pensions, a bold stroke which was too much for his new colleagues, and even in his Tariff

Reform campaign he was always concerned to show that his policy was of benefit to all the community.

On tariff revision, he had been prepared to think about Britain's trading position back in the 1880s, and his later challenge to the orthodoxy of Free Trade was not a totally new departure. Similarly, on foreign affairs, there is a continuity in his broad approach; he had never been Internationalist of the John Bright Radical school as far as Britain's position in the world was concerned. Indeed, in his desire to stand up for the rights of Englishmen, he echoed a very Palmerstonian spirit. Not for nothing did Lord Granville describe him in Gladstone's Second Ministry as 'almost the greatest jingo in the Cabinet'.

On Ireland, from an early stage, his opposition to any notion of separatism was clear, for he believed passionately in the integrity of the United Kingdom. Committed as he was to increasing Britain's influence in the rest of the world, he could never reconcile this with Home Rule for Ireland.

His was a developing mind, and like any forward-looking statesmen he was willing to change course as the occasion merited. New facts and new forces demand different responses, and yesterday's solutions can become irrelevant. To accuse him of changing his outlook to suit his own ambitions may seem rather harsh on a man who left the Liberal Party in 1886 precisely because he could not accept its new policy of Home Rule. As he taunted them in later years; 'It is you who have changed, and not I'. In leaving it, he was bound to sacrifice many friendships and jeopardise his chance of securing the leadership when Gladstone retired.

To say, as his critics often did, that he changed his mind to buy votes is only to say that he was a politician who realised that to achieve his objectives he needed popular support. Others who held different views were nevertheless not in the business of repelling popularity!

His broad objectives remained consistent; it was his tactics and particular policies which changed. In his later phase, he was waging a more defensive struggle against the New Radicals whom he saw as a threat to social stability even though he himself had been accused of posing a danger to the owners of wealth and property early in his career. Yesterday's Radical had become today's Unionist; it was not the time now to urge his supporters on to more Radical goals.

If the Irish felt he was a Judas and many Liberals could never forgive him for splitting the party, some others were more charitable. Even though he became an arch political enemy, Lloyd George still had some regard for his old erstwhile hero. He and Chamberlain had some things in common, especially in their political approach. As Lucy Masterman later wrote of the Welshman:

> he was the least doctrinaire of men, as little as Mr Chamberlain
> . . . he stands in the furrow that Chamberlain deserted.

Points to consider

1) He was not a popular member of the House of Commons in the early days after his election. Why was this?

2) In what ways did he make an impact on the Liberal Party in the years spent in Opposition, 1876–80?

3) What evidence is there of his Radical attitudes whilst he was President of the Board of Trade?

4) Why was he unable to reunite with the Liberals after the schism of 1886?

5) What factors inclined him towards the Conservative Party of Lord Salisbury in the late 1800s?

6) What impression do you form of his relations with Gladstone?

7) How did Lord Salisbury and Chamberlain regard each other?

8) What were his main political beliefs at the time of his entry into Parliament, and how far did he modify them in his later career?

9) How much stronger was his position as a Cabinet Minister in 1895 than in 1880?

10) Was he really too radical for the late nineteenth century Conservative Party?

11) Is he open to the charges of opportunism and inconsistency in his political career? Are these necessarily defects in a prominent politician?

3

CHARACTER AND RELATIONSHIPS

By the time he entered the House of Commons, Joseph Chamberlain's fame had spread widely. He was no longer just 'Brummagem Joe', but a nationally well-known figure in the Liberal Party. Many of its members admired his drive and effectiveness, but that was by no means the effect he had on everyone. Throughout his life he aroused remarkably strong admiration and animosity; while he gained power, applause and fame, he was also the victim of personal attacks of extraordinary bitterness. What sort of man was he, and why did he evoke such intense reactions?

In appearance, he was small and neat and carefully dressed, sporting a monocle and an orchid in his lapel. The eyeglass and the flower, both of which first appeared in his early debating days, were the most distinctive features of his image, readily seized upon by the political cartoonists of the day.

His manner often seemed cold and chilling, though this may have been a protective mask worn only in public life, one which concealed many periods of great personal sadness. Though he possessed many valuable qualities, many felt it was perhaps easier to admire than to like him. He could be brash and pushy, often extremely provocative in speech, and his obvious ambition and self-confidence were not moderated by obvious consideration for the reactions of anyone else.

He easily took offence, yet Beatrice Potter noted that his 'intense sensitiveness to his own wrongs was not tempered by a corresponding sensitivity to the feelings and rights of others'. Chamberlain had a two-year relationship with her, and though attracted by his personality, she was often infuriated by him. Her comments often reflect this irritation, but they do also usefully reinforce his reputation for insensitivity and overconfidence.

His vanity and self-righteousness, his natural frankness and pugnacity were also not endearing attributes, and opponents disliked the way he rode roughshod over their views, trampling any objections underfoot. His earnestness and sobriety of manner, his unimpassioned but pointed and incisive tone of speech, though perhaps less open to criticism, hardly lent any warmth to the gloomy impression.

Yet there was also a very positive side to his character. He was industrious and determined; if there was a job to be done, he was single minded in tackling it. An optimist in his approach to problems, he was certain they could be overcome. He dealt with issues shrewdly and energetically, with the full confidence that his solution was the most appropriate.

He was not an idealist, nor was he a man of imagination who dreamed inspiring and uplifting dreams. He was not a cultivated intellectual, nor a man of obvious literary and artistic talents. Above all he was a singularly pragmatic, clear-headed businessman who saw issues in uncomplicated terms and had the ability to explain them to the public in a straightforward manner.

He was not renowned for considering other people's feelings and opinions, nor did he try to achieve his object by subtle or conciliatory means. As he put it:

> on every committee of thirteen, there are twelve who go to the meeting having given no thought to the subject and are prepared to accept someone else's lead. One goes, having made up his mind what he means shall be done. I always make it my business to be that one.

This remark gives a useful insight into his methods. Above all, he would drive on, in the face of whatever opposition. It is not surprising that his relations with so many people were marked by mistrust and antagonism. He saw himself as a man who knew where he was going, and saw others as less clear-cut in their ideas. Thus, in his view, they needed to be led by someone with a firm grasp of events, one free of doubts or second thoughts.

From the earliest days, many politicians could recognise his capacity and potential; as Gladstone said, 'Mr. Chamberlain's character is remarkable, as are, in high degree, his talents'. They were impressed by his forceful and dynamic approach, but were nevertheless wary of him. He never sought to woo their support and was often scornful of their ability. He was a difficult colleague and an implacable opponent, and, in the words of the historian A.J.P. Taylor, 'unsparing in victory, and savage in defeat'.

Those on Chamberlain's own side of politics often experienced the acerbic and critical nature of his observations. The lethargy of Hartington's leadership led to Chamberlain comparing him to Rip Van Winkle, the fictional character who slept for twenty years. Gladstone was earlier attacked for his preoccupation with translating classical works and writing pamphlets:

> an ex-Minister who devotes his leisure to a critical examination of the querulousness of an aged priest is hardly in sympathy with the robust good sense of English Liberalism.

Particularly in the later years of his career, colleagues also found him lacking in loyalty. Lady Frances Balfour was to comment of his role in Tory Cabinets; 'it is not that he is disloyal, but he does not understand or observe the rules of the game'. Of course, he was not of the usual gentlemanly breed that graced Conservative administrations, and for him politics was far too serious to be ever viewed as a game. Chamberlain was not the man to worry about accepted conventions as to how senior politicians should react.

In fact, Joseph Chamberlain, man of Birmingham, a self-made Victorian success, was not a man ever to feel fully at home in a party where Whig grandees or Tory landowners had a dominant influence. Such people didn't share his preoccupation with political life. Beatrice Potter later observed that:

> The political creed is the whole man, the outcome of his peculiar physical and mental temperament, played upon by the experiences of his life.

ON THE PUBLIC PLATFORM
—

Back in his early days in the local debating society, he revealed no obvious gift for speechmaking. His contributions were formal and because they were carefully learnt by heart, they came across as unnatural set-pieces. He spoke clearly, but certainly was no orator; his approach was workmanlike and effective, but his style lacked passion. Disraeli unflatteringly compared them to those of a 'cheesemonger'.

In his maiden speech in the House of Commons, he was more informal in style and, from then on quickly improved. He gained in self-assurance, and in his prime became a really accomplished performer. He planned his set-pieces carefully and ensured that they always had a clear theme. Because three or four days were involved in preparation of each, he rationed their number.

His style was forthright and vigorous, his manner earnest, but especially in his Radical days, it was the sharpness of his tone which made his speeches memorable. He was no respecter of reputations, and he would launch into the most bitter and contemptuous assaults on those whose attitudes and behaviour stood in his way. Naturally belligerent on the attack, he could respond devastatingly when challenged. Richard Jay, in his biography, has vividly described his manner when in full cry;

> His characteristic sally was the sneer, delivered with a poker face, broken by a distinct curl of the lip.

Yet, if the content was sharp and unsparing, he could arouse his audience to great enthusiasm.

> Into the tones of his voice, he threw the warmth and feeling which was lacking in his words, and every thought, every feeling, the slightest intonation of irony and contempt was reflected in the face of the crowd.

His Birmingham supporters knew his ways:

> the variations of inflection, the pauses for effect, the sparing of gestures. He had a trick of passing his forefinger by his nose just before he made a joke. The people of Birmingham, with the benefit of years of observation, would burst into laughter before the words had left his lips. He hammered at two or three conclusions, reached by different avenues, illustrated with telling examples, and so skilfully presented that the argument seemed irresistible. (David Dilks, *Neville Chamberlain*)

HOME AND FAMILY LIFE

Until 1880, Joseph Chamberlain lived at Southborne, a large residence in the Birmingham district of Edgbaston, but in that year he moved closer to his constituency. His new house, Highbury, built of red brick and in gothic style, was at Moor Green. It took its name from the family home at Highbury Place in London, and it was a building with so many rooms that it was ideal for bringing up what had become a large family. It was conveniently close to the relatives and the Unitarians with whom they mixed, and suitably spacious for entertaining them.

Outside, the setting of woods and water was pleasant and relaxing. The gardens were lovingly cared for, and, of course, there were greenhouses for the growing of his beloved orchids, Again, Beatrice Potter was less than impressed. Given a guided tour of the orchid house, she caused offence by observing her preference for wildflowers!

The residence was entirely suitable for a successful self-made Victorian destined for higher things. Joseph Chamberlain controlled the household and family and visitors (other than Beatrice Potter) fawned upon him.

There was often a formality about home life and meals, a generally subdued air. As in the days of his own upbringing, there could be fun and sparkling conversation in the family home, but overall the dominant character of Chamberlain dictated the terms of enjoyment.

Food and drink were available in abundance, for the religious Nonconformity of the family was surprisingly never associated with a need to avoid alcoholic liquor. A comfortable way of life was much to Chamberlain's taste, and he never felt the necessity to balance excessive consumption with much exercise. Indeed, he remarked that more people died as a result of taking exercise than from any other cause. When invited to give his recipe for perpetual youth, the answer was 'to take no exercise and smoke all day'.

Family life was much affected by his ill-fortune in marriage. To lose one wife in childbirth was a very sad blow, to lose two in such circumstances was both unusual and a great personal tragedy. His first wife Harriet bore him two children, Beatrice and Joseph Austen, in the short period of their happy life together. Florence, Harriet's cousin, quieter and more reserved, was loyal and subservient, and was content to play a subordinate role to her husband whom she tried very hard to please. They had four children, Neville, Ida, Hilda and Ethel and Florence made no distinction between her own offspring and the children of the first marriage.

Over them all presided Joseph Chamberlain who expected his women to be supportive and always present to help him entertain his guests. From his children, he expected and received respect, truthfulness, discipline and unquestioning obedience; they knew that they were expected to meet his exacting standards, and felt somewhat in awe of him. His relations with them were marked by a coolness, only occasionally relieved by flashes of emotion. He wasn't easily able to demonstrate love and affection, and as a man so dedicated to his work, his attention to their interests was spasmodic. It was to the aunt, Joseph's sister, that they looked for the warmth that he was unable to give them.

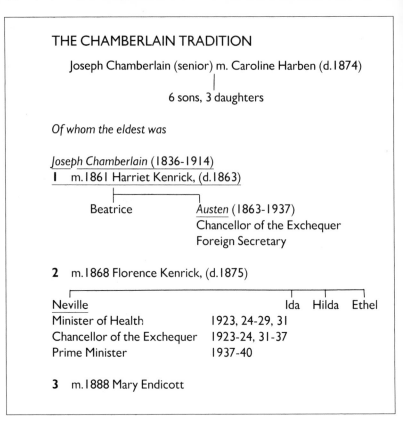

THE CHAMBERLAIN TRADITION

Joseph Chamberlain (senior) m. Caroline Harben (d. 1874)

6 sons, 3 daughters

Of whom the eldest was

Joseph Chamberlain (1836-1914)
1   m. 1861 Harriet Kenrick, (d. 1863)

Beatrice   Austen (1863-1937)
                   Chancellor of the Exchequer
                   Foreign Secretary

2   m. 1868 Florence Kenrick, (d. 1875)

Neville   Ida   Hilda   Ethel
Minister of Health   1923, 24-29, 31
Chancellor of the Exchequer   1923-24, 31-37
Prime Minister   1937-40

3   m. 1888 Mary Endicott

During their childhood, Chamberlain never spoke to his first two children about their mother. Later in life, when his father was about to marry for the third time, Austen referred to this long silence with his father, Chamberlain's reply was significant;

> Until happiness came again into my life, I did not dare to – and even now I can't do it without the tears coming into my eyes.

He could not speak of her without losing his composure. The son felt that he was a constant reminder of his father's great personal loss, for it was just after his birth that Harriet had died.

Florence died whilst her husband was Mayor of Birmingham, and her death made him immerse himself even more in his duties. Within a few months of Florence's death, his mother also died, and it is hardly surprising that he temporarily lapsed into deep despondency. Personal sadness made him withdraw into himself, deepening a reserve which was already there.

Neville Chamberlain later commented that 'under an exterior that for many years was rather hard and cold . . . (he) concealed intensely strong feelings'. These feelings were not revealed to the world beyond his private thoughts.

Despite the strength of his own Unitarian connections, and his own past involvement in church and Sunday-school life, he lost his faith. As he later wrote to Dilke;

> The death of my first wife brought the whole thing very close to me and the doctrines which did very well before broke down under the calamity.

He lost any interest in church attendance and was content, as an atheist, to concentrate on making life on earth as bearable as possible rather than to speculate on the prospects of 'what is to come afterwards'.

By the time he reached the onset of his ministerial career, he had been forced to come to terms with private grief and, as a widower, no longer found consolation in his religious life. His tendency towards seriousness, left him prone to spells of gloom and depression like that which had overcome him in 1876. He never found it easy to relax and as a normal domestic life was no longer immediately available, he devoted himself to his political activity, throwing himself energetically into his public life. The political creed was 'the whole man'; the Chamberlain that the public saw was very similar to the one known to his family and friends.

REMARRIAGE
—

His second widowhood lasted for more than twelve years, and towards the end of it he formed a relationship with Beatrice Potter. She was wealthy and attractive, with a strong interest in social problems and the ways in which local government could tackle them. She was fascinated by him and for a time passionately in love, noting that he possessed 'energy and personal magnetism, in a word masculine force, to an almost superlative degree'.

However, she found other aspects of his character difficult to accept, for she recognised his strong desire to dominate, whether in politics or within the household at Highbury. Guests dining at his home tended to massage his ego, and she was irked by the subservience of the females around him. As Beatrice herself possessed a wilful and highly individual personality, and obvious intelligence, she realised that he was seeking an altogether more submissive person who would not challenge his beliefs, but would support his endeavours. The relationship petered out, and she later married Sidney Webb who was certainly not endowed with Chamberlain's domineering 'masculine force' to any noticeable degree. She could exert her own desire for mastery over him, and develop a shared interest in municipal reform and Fabian Socialism.

By contrast, Mary Endicott, the daughter of an American Cabinet Minister, aged only 24 when Chamberlain met her, was the ideal partner for him. She was happy to play the supporting role, and possessed the charm, good looks and intelligence which made her an excellent hostess.

She and Chamberlain had met whilst he was on his American visit, and after a short romance fell much in love. He returned to England to report on his political negotiations, and prepare his home and family for her arrival.

In November 1888, they were married in Washington DC, and on Christmas Eve they arrived back in Birmingham. She easily fitted into Highbury life, and Chamberlain seemed much more relaxed after marrying her. In turn, this helped him relate to his children. Though she was younger than either Beatrice or Austen, they had no difficulty in accepting her, and the daughter remarked that 'she unlocked his heart and we were able to enter in as never before'. She fulfilled the role he wanted, and in his eyes was a perfect wife and mother. Within London society she was equally successful; Queen Victoria was greatly impressed, remarking: 'Mrs Chamberlain looked lovely, and was as charming as ever'.

In personal terms, he had found satisfaction, and his third wife was to sustain him for the rest of his life.

4

MAYOR OF BIRMINGHAM, 1873-6

Birmingham developed rapidly at the time of the Industrial Revolution and the problems of unplanned, haphazard growth could only be solved by an effective response from local leaders. Since 1838, it had been a municipal corporation, with the town council responsible for providing services. By the 1860s, however, much social provision was urgently needed. It could not be much longer delayed for, as the business life of the city expanded, the importance of pulling down the slums and rebuilding was pressing. An improved road network, water supply and drainage system were essential if expansion was to occur in such a way that Birmingham became a place of which its inhabitants could feel proud.

Chamberlain was to employ his considerable vision and drive to tackle the problems confronting the Council. His business experience and forceful manner made him the ideal person to assume command, and the position of Mayor offered much scope for his dominant personality. The holder of the office did not only act as a Chairman of the Council. He was entitled to attend every Committee meeting, and this gave him a key role in coordinating Council policy, offering advice and mediating in any disputes.

From the beginning, Chamberlain had a clear idea of what he wanted to achieve, and this extract from his first address as Mayor reflects his deep feeling for the borough:

> Birmingham is not my native town, but it is the town of my adoption and predilection; I have lived here about twenty years and I think it is the finest, the most intelligent, the most patriotic town on the face of the universe, and I am prepared to maintain the same opinion before any audience, in or out of Birmingham. At the same time, my favourite town, I admit it with grief and sorrow, is not perfect.

He went on to venture the prophecy that 'The town shall not, with God's help, know itself'.

A few municipalities had already begun to demolish their slums whilst others were beginning to set up public utilities for sanitation and other services. In the three years of the Chamberlain mayoralty, Birmingham acquired two major utilities, a programme of slum clearance and a main thoroughfare.

'GAS AND WATER SOCIALISM'

The first major scheme he embarked upon was to bring about a municipal gas supply. This was not a new idea; Manchester had had one since 1817. But Chamberlain had been contemplating the idea since becoming a councillor in 1869 and now employed several arguments in support of the proposal, some ideological, others practical.

He strongly believed that utilities such as gas, on which everyone depended, should be in the hands of the elected representatives of the people, and so run for the public good rather than for the private gain of a few individuals. Moreover, municipal services would enhance the prestige and power of the Council and, in addition, prove a highly profitable undertaking. His political opponents emphasised the short-term debt which would increase from £½m-£2½m, whilst the private gas companies were inevitably hostile to being taken over.

The scheme was approved in 1875 and given Parliamentary authorisation the following year. Chamberlain's stress on the profitability of the venture soon proved to be justified, for a profit of £34,000 was made within a year of taking over the private supplies. Over the next few years, the municipal enterprise was very lucrative and by 1884 had made nearly £¼m. The consumer was also better served for prices had been reduced by 30% in the same period.

THE WATER ISSUE

This successful gas enterprise was seen as a way of providing the funds for other improvements, and Chamberlain's intention was to acquire the water supply in a similar manner. A supply of pure water was obviously necessary for the health of the population, but the exercise might prove costly. By tackling the profitable gas takeover first, enough money was generated to finance the next stage of his plans.

Again, in planning a scheme for municipalised water, Chamberlain was not pioneering a new idea. Leeds, Manchester, Cardiff, Glasgow and Dublin had all owned their own water supplies for some time, and in the decade before 1870 a number of other places had followed suit. In Birmingham, there was need for action, for although the Birmingham Water Works Company provided a supply in parts of the city for three days a week, there were still 15,000 people dependent on wells.

Chamberlain felt that, in sanitary terms, the situation was unacceptable and wanted to remove the dangers associated with people using discoloured and polluted water, 'as bad as sewage before clarification'. He drew attention to the connection between impure water and disease, and claimed that people who lacked any adequate means of supply were driven to stealing it from the Company taps in the vicinity. Again, as with gas, he stressed that monopoly utilities which were basic to the needs of everyone in the community should not be controlled by private speculators. Moreover, the Council was not looking for a profit to be made because cheaper water for all was desirable as a priority:

> Whereas there should be a profit made on the gas undertaking, the waterworks should never be a source of profit, as all profit should go in the price of water.

In municipal hands, the water supply was increased and over the next few years the use of many wells was discontinued because they were found to be so contaminated by sewage. The result of Chamberlain's enterprise was a notable reduction in disease and in the death rates, though in 1889 a writer in the *Birmingham Mail* mentioned another advantage:

> Without the additions that have been made, the town would have been a desert of Sahara, while the Edgbaston horticulturalists would have been reduced to the necessity of moistening their lawns with beer.

Also basic to improvements in public health was an improved system of inspection and more expert advice. As a result of Gladstonian legislation, all sanitary authorities in large towns had to employ a Medical Officer of Health, which Birmingham had done since 1872. A Drainage Board was also set up to supervise the safe disposal of sewage. The combination of such measures and vigorous leadership did much to make Birmingham a healthier place in which to live. However, it was Chamberlain's Town Improvement Scheme, involving the demolition of some of the most squalid and insanitary housing, for which his Mayoralty is most remembered.

THE IMPROVEMENT SCHEME

In 1875, Disraeli's Conservative Government passed an Artisans' and Labourers' Dwellings Improvement Act, drawn up by Richard Cross, the Home Secretary, and the President of the Local Government Board, George Sclater-Booth. The measure gave local authorities the right of compulsory purchase of slum land and financial assistance to clear and redevelop affected areas. Chamberlain had already been in touch with Cross during the preparatory stages of the bill, and had discussed the scope it allowed for a major programme of clearance and rebuilding in Birmingham.

As a keen supporter of the Cross legislation, Chamberlain soon established a local Improvement Committee charged with the task of drawing up a scheme which would remove slums. He personally acted as Counsel for the Corporation at the public enquiry, and persuasively argued that bad housing was a serious health hazard, harbouring disease and contributing to a high rate of premature death. While such conditions existed, he argued, it was impossible to effect an improvement in public health.

Under the plan he put forward to the Council, the Improvement Area included some 93 acres between the railway stations at New Street and Snow Hill, and Aston Street. It covered appalling slum areas like Rope Walk and Lower Priory, but also some superior Georgian housing, and involved taking 43½ acres into municipal control. The aim was to create a new thoroughfare through the worst territory, a road which Chamberlain referred to as a 'boulevard' on the Parisian model. It would cut through the existing street pattern and be constructed on a grand scale, nearly 1½ kilometres in length and 20 metres wide.

He told the Council that the annual cost of slum conditions was far higher than that of the proposed venture. He estimated the outlay at just under £1½m, and believed that approximately half that sum could be clawed back by sales and letting charges on the new property with its higher rateable value. Overall, the burden on ratepayers would be about £12,000 a year, substantially less than the profit being registered by his new gas enterprise.

The Birmingham slums before the Improvement Scheme was carried out – a typical street scene in 1876

Is that too heavy a burden for the town of Birmingham to contemplate for such an improvement as that proposed? I believe the town, and, above all, the next generation, will have cause to bless the Town Council of Birmingham if it carries the scheme before it, and exercises what I venture to call a sagacious audacity.

Opposition to the Improvement Scheme

Chamberlain was bent upon an ambitious scheme of civic improvement. He brushed aside objections to his vision in his characteristic manner. He had an ability to strike at the root of the problem, and he worked with such energy and alacrity that his opponents were outwitted. Sensing possible difficulties or sources of opposition, he was resourceful in overriding them.

Not surprisingly, he encountered much antagonism from the owners of slum dwellings and also from those who owned the more desirable properties in the vicinity of New Street and Old Square. It was alleged that he was using the Cross Act in a way which had never been envisaged; rather than removing the slums and bringing about an improvement in sanitation, Chamberlain was set upon a costly and prestigious municipal development.

The local Conservatives were dismissive of the proposals, coming as they did from Chamberlain and other 'wild and radical' elements within the Liberal Party. As one local observer put it:

They fought the scheme tooth and nail. They racked their brains for arguments against it, they contrived and schemed at every turn to wreck it. The town echoed with noise of wordy combat . . . For it was a Chamberlain scheme, and must, therefore be vile and ruinous and pernicious and wicked and against the constitution and the scriptures, and – well, it was a damnable scheme.

The necessary enabling Bill was approved in August 1876 while Chamberlain was still Mayor, and work began two years later. It was to be another six years before Aston Street was reached and his reputation was often called in question during that time. The 'Rue Chamberlain' or 'Chamberlain's folly', was a gift to the satirists of the day who, from the beginning, were at pains to point out that the exact route of Corporation Street was imprecisely outlined.

It was the cost of the project, however, which was often scorned and, whenever difficulties arose, as in 1881, the opposition sharply intensified.

Chamberlain himself noted in 1877, that 'there were some of our political opponents who actually rejoiced at the prospect of a financial failure, which might have plunged the town and the Council into severe embarrassment'. *The Dart*, a local newspaper, organised a poetry competition on the scheme and, among the largely critical offerings, the following contribution summed up the views of some of the doubters;

> Didn't we gird at the street of J.C.
> and say its promoters were silly uns?
> we dubbed it the acme of absurdity
> and objected to throw away millions.
> It has been a dear bargain, there can be no doubt
> And we say it without hesitation
> Its a drain on our means we would well be without
> Is this boulevard of our Corporation!

In the early stages, the builders paid good prices for buildings fronting onto Corporation Street, though areas to the rear went cheaply and several lots failed even to reach the reserve price. Times were hard in the late 1870s as the recession hit business confidence, and it was easy to deride a massive speculative venture. Yet Chamberlain eventually had reason to be well satisfied with his plans for, by 1892, there was no longer an annual deficit and the 'boulevard' was paying for itself. The term may seem pretentious for the thoroughfare which, though wide, was treeless and contained a variety of architectural styles. Nevertheless, many of the new buildings, especially at the New Street end, were tasteful, with impressive frontages, and there was general approval of their appearance.

By the end of the decade, the death rates within the improved area had fallen dramatically, but critics could muster at least one explanation for this. *The Dart* noted:

> New Birmingham recipe for lowering the death rate of an insanitary area. Pull down nearly all the houses and make the inhabitants move somewhere else. 'Tis an excellent plan and I'll tell you for why. Where there's no person living, no person can die.

There was some point in the flippant observation, for it soon became apparent that there were nearly 4000 fewer artisans' dwellings than there had been before the slums had been cleared. No new houses had been constructed, which is perhaps surprising as Chamberlain had often dwelt on the evils of poor housing which so degraded the lives of its inhabitants.

Corporation Street at the turn of the century

However, the 1875 Act did not require municipalities to build new accommodation and moreover, special authorisation from the Local Government Board was needed before they could construct working class houses. Birmingham was slow to seek such approval, and when eventually dwellings were erected they were mainly in the suburbs, with only a few ever being built in the Improvement Area.

OTHER DEVELOPMENTS

In his three years as Mayor, Chamberlain busied himself with transforming many aspects of Birmingham life. He carried a resolution that new Assize Courts should be built at the less fashionable end of Corporation Street, a proposal that would improve the tone of that section by creating attractive properties of obvious use to the town. The result was the construction of the Birmingham Law Courts, and this handsome building set a standard which was to be followed in this part of the boulevard.

He was very active in the sphere of education and as Chairman of the School Board initiated an extensive school building programme which meant that by 1877 some 70 per cent of children attended school regularly compared with only 28 per cent when the School Board began its work.

The central and branch libraries, an art gallery, municipal swimming baths, new parks and gardens, better street lighting and modern paving are a legacy of these years. Chamberlain, never one to underestimate his contribution, was well aware of the scale of his achievement when he told his friend, Jesse Collings:

> I think I have almost completed my municipal programme and may sing 'Nunc Dimittis'. The town will be Parked, Paved, Assized, Marketed, Gas-and-Watered, and Improved, all as the result of three years active work and with the general approval of the great bulk of the ratepayers.

Prominent in the local temperance movement, he was determined that Corporation Street would not be ruined by public houses or other licensed premises. Furthermore, he interested himself in a scheme for municipal control of all public houses, believing that this would help curb drunkenness and also yield a useful profit. However, when as an MP his private member's bill on the issue failed, this particular project was abandoned.

LOCAL REACTIONS

Nonetheless, the Chamberlain Mayoralty was a remarkable success story for, inspired by his relentless determination and ambition, Birmingham had become a model of sound local government. Indeed, in the 1890s, an American observer was to describe it as 'the best governed city in the world'.

Of course, the very backwardness of Birmingham's facilities and the inertia of its administration in the middle of the century made the situation ripe for change, and the prosperity of the early 1870s provided the essential confidence for a period of civic enterprise.

Inevitably, Chamberlain made enemies; some, even on his own side, resented his forceful style and Chamberlain knew this. As he explained to Jesse Collings in 1876 'I had to use my despotic authority a little in arriving at the estimates'. Others, more seriously, noted how the Chamberlains had bought up property in the Improvement Area, thus making it easy to push through the programme of demolition and reconstruction – and also themselves gaining some financial advantage in the venture.

Moreover, he was not alone in his efforts to modernise the town of his adoption. There were many other able and visionary figures who were committed to the civic gospel and were ready to see massive social advance and whose work was overshadowed by the dominating Chamberlain. However, whatever may be said about his methods and tactics, or the contribution of others, the beneficial effect of his work is difficult to challenge.

It was to his credit that he seized the opportunity presented, and provided the drive and leadership for such a transformation. His energetic approach to municipal reform made many people believe in his plan to make Birmingham a pleasant, modern, well-governed borough.

Because of his reputation as a shrewd businessman, many people in Birmingham trusted his judgement. He was therefore able to rally popular support, including that of the all-important ratepayers, in favour of his initiatives. They were impressed by his efforts and subsequently showed him a remarkable degree of loyalty throughout the vicissitudes of his often stormy political life. The monument erected next to the Town Hall in 1880 was a token of their gratitude, and he was justly proud of such recognition.

In March 1888, an honour was offered which he was pleased to accept. Birmingham made him a Freeman of the town, the first citizen to be so rewarded. It was a suitable tribute to his contribution to the borough, and it was fitting also that John Bright the great Liberal of the 1840s and 50s should speak on his behalf – the last public speech Bright ever made.

Whether as a member of the Council or later as an MP, Chamberlain was committed to the 'town of (his) adoption'. He remained true to that promise (given in 1873), for the Birmingham of the late nineteenth century was a vastly different place from the one whose weaknesses he had earlier diagnosed. His achievements gave a new boost to the cause of local government, and Birmingham became a model of progressive administration. As a contemporary explained;

> Municipal reformers were looking to Birmingham, as the eyes of the faithful are turned towards Mecca.

Points to consider

1) **What picture emerges of Chamberlain's personal qualities of leadership during his Mayoralty?**
2) **In Birmingham as Mayor and at other points in his career, why did he arouse such opposition to his plans?**
3) **As he moved onto the national scene in 1876, his verdict on his period as Mayor was rather self-congratulatory in tone. Does he deserve the credit he gave himself? Which of his achievements do you find admirable?**

5

RADICALISM: OPPOSITION AND OFFICE 1876-86

Lord Hartington, a Whig grandee, had become the new Liberal Leader in 1875. His appointment confirmed Chamberlain's view that the party was an unnatural creation, with Whigs of great social standing at the top and convinced Radicals underneath. He wanted to reconstruct it around a more left-wing programme which would require 'a more cordial and thorough union between the nonconformists and the working classes'.

He had explained his basic philosophy in 1874:

> I am a Radical Reformer because I would reform and remove ignorance, poverty, intemperance and crime at their very roots. What is the cause of all this ignorance and vice? Many people say that intemperance is at the bottom of everything, and I am not inclined to disagree with them . . . (But) intemperance itself is only an effect produced by causes that lie deeper still. I should say that these causes, in the first place, are the gross ignorance of the masses; and, in the second place, the horrible, shameful homes in which many of the poor are forced to live.

Whereas he then felt it was 'ridiculous to talk of temperance to men who have every reason to leave their homes', his attitude had changed by 1876, the year of his entry to the House of Commons. Temperance reform was of much concern to his Nonconformist supporters, and he now saw it as the issue central to all other social and political questions. Though, despite his Unitarian background, he had a liking for alcohol himself, he was well aware of the evils of drunkenness and its effects on the lives of the poor.

He also felt deeply about corporal punishment. He always opposed any form of physical cruelty, and was active in the opposition to a government bill allowing flogging for breaches of military discipline. Such punishment was 'degrading, brutal, cruel and unworthy of our civilisation', a viewpoint which brought him into conflict with the leadership of the Liberal Party. He refused to modify his attitude as Hartington wanted him to do, but in the end it was leader himself who tabled an unsuccessful motion to abolish flogging in the services. The incident shows that senior figures in the party saw the importance of appeasing an influential Radical.

At other times during the Disraeli premiership, his public and parliamentary speeches covered a wide spectrum of issues. They ranged from support for free elementary education to extending the franchise, from the need for female teachers to local government reform. Debates in the House exposed divisions in the Radical contingent at Westminster, and Chamberlain had a low view of such disunity. He was also unimpressed by the state of party organisation in the country.

THE BULGARIAN ATROCITIES AND THE NLF

The government's handling of the question of the Bulgarian massacres and its supine pro-Turkish policy provided the Liberal opposition with an ideal opportunity to denounce their conduct of affairs. As news came through about the activities of the Turkish Bashi-Bazouks in ruthlessly crushing the Bulgarian risings, Disraeli tried to minimise the horrors. Many Liberals believed his policy to be utterly cynical and immoral, and Gladstone's active conscience was aroused by the iniquities of Ottoman rule. For him it was a great moral issue, and he emerged from retirement to put down a resolution condemning government policy. Few leading Liberals backed him, but Chamberlain became much involved in Gladstone's highly personal campaign.

There was some bravery on Chamberlain's part in associating himself with what seemed to be a pro-Russian stance over Bulgaria and the Near Eastern question. Gladstone realised this, and was grateful for Chamberlain's support, even though he suspected his motives. Chamberlain was certainly anxious to show that his Radicalism was not just concerned with domestic issues but also had an ethical dimension; this would help to broaden the basis of his political backing. However, he was not personally much attracted by the 'politics of passion', and could never aspire to match Gladstone when it came to moral denunciations.

The public excitement over Bulgaria, and the government's increasing economic difficulties, convinced Chamberlain that the time was ripe to unite all Liberal Associations by forming a National Liberal Federation. He was determined that Birmingham, rather than London, would be the headquarters, seeing that this would strengthen his hand against the Whigs in the party. Also, if the Birmingham association became the model for the new organisation, it would help cement the links between the Liberal Party and the recently enfranchised voters; on the six-hundred-strong central committee in Birmingham, Chamberlain claimed that at least three-quarters were from the working classes.

Chamberlain's relations with Gladstone, never easy, had temporarily improved, and realising the extent of Gladstone's reputation and prestige, he wanted to associate him with the formation of the NLF. He invited him to Birmingham to address a meeting at Bingley Hall. Gladstone accepted, seeing the occasion as another chance to address a large crowd on the evils of Disraelian foreign policy. He had reservations about some of the other arrangements which Chamberlain planned, such as a tour of Birmingham's municipal achievements, but eventually agreed to come.

Gladstone did briefly endorse the NLF as Chamberlain had hoped, and the meeting overwhelmingly backed the new organisation. According to Chamberlain, its official aim was to provide a democratic forum through which the Liberals could discuss policy. It would also help to secure a common purpose among Liberal Associations. Within the party, many suspected another motive; they saw it as the bid of an ambitious politician to assume greater control over party policy and organisation. The charge was again made that he was seeking to Americanise British political life by the creation of another caucus.

THE RADICALS AND GLADSTONE

Radicals such as Chamberlain had mixed feelings about Gladstone. On social matters, his attitudes were seen as a barrier to the development of a more constructive policy. Gladstone was unconvinced that state action could alleviate poverty, remove the slums, extend rights to labour or tackle other social evils. Reflecting traditional Liberal ideas of laissez-faire, he emphasised personal effort, thrift and self-help, the qualities by which individuals could improve themselves. Chamberlain also saw great merit in individual initiative, but nonetheless believed that legislative action had a role, particularly in destroying privilege and class barriers.

On constitutional matters, such as extending the vote and the secret ballot, Gladstone's record was much more in line with the Radical viewpoint. However, it was the question of the Bulgarian Atrocities that gave the Radicals at Westminster a new lease of life. This was an issue to rally round, and it was the dominant figure of Gladstone who had provided the lead. When he launched his Midlothian Campaigns in 1879-80, his value as an electioneering asset was obvious to them all.

In 1880, faced with a growing business and agrarian depression, and Gladstone's onslaughts on his overseas policy, Disraeli dissolved Parliament and called an election. This was to be the only time that Chamberlain was ever forced to fight for his seat in Birmingham, and he campaigned with his usual vigour. He was attacked by his opponents with great ferocity, for he had made enemies in the town. Some of these were looking for an opportunity to take him down a peg, and were pleased to see that, though elected, he came only third among the Liberal candidates. Though he was peeved by the result, he was still nearly 4000 votes clear of the strongest Conservative challenger. Moreover, the Liberal party as a whole did well in the elections, and gained a handsome victory.

The NLF was active in 60 constituencies, in several of which seats were gained from the Conservatives. Chamberlain was convinced that the organisation, fired by his Radical zeal, had played a major part in the result. He now expected his reward from the new Prime Minister, Gladstone. Chamberlain was glad to see him back, for, as he told Dilke in 1876:

> I can't help feeling he is our best card . . . If he were to come back for a few years (he can't continue in public life for very much longer) he would probably do much for us and pave the way for me.

CABINET OFFICE UNDER GLADSTONE 1880-85

The Radicals were determined to gain some recognition in the Gladstone Government, seeing the election victory as a direct result of their contribution. Chamberlain wrote to his friend, Dilke, another rising star in the Liberal Party, suggesting a compact by which neither of them would serve in the new administration unless they were both offered suitable posts.

Dilke agreed, though he believed that only one of them would be in the Cabinet.

Chamberlain played a subtle role in the period of Cabinet formation, skilfully seizing opportunities to promote his interests. By stressing his popularity in the English boroughs, he also implied that if his importance was not recognised then he might organise Radical opinion in the House and outside, and might even consider running separate Radical candidates in local elections.

Gladstone wanted a Cabinet with familiar faces in it, some belonging to friends, others to loyal members of the party. He was more at ease with proven supporters, and wanted a predominantly Whig administration. He accepted that token Radical representation was necessary, but had no wish to give a Cabinet position to anyone who had not previously held ministerial office.

However, after the interventions of Harcourt and Bright, he concluded that it was better to have Chamberlain in the Cabinet where he might be more easily contained. Otherwise, as an independently minded backbencher, he might cause trouble whenever the Radicals disapproved of the Government's handling of events. He realised that Chamberlain was widely seen as a spokesman for Radicalism and Nonconformity, and, because of the NLF, as a key figure in the party's organisation. Therefore, he reluctantly made him President of the Board of Trade. John Bright was the only other Radical in the Cabinet.

From the start, Gladstone's leadership was less clear and decisive than was necessary to achieve any cohesion in the Ministry. Within the party he was undoubtedly a towering figure, probably the only person who could keep it together. To the Radicals, he made the overwhelmingly Whig Government acceptable, for his presence seemed to offer the chance of moderate reform. To the Whigs, he was a bastion against the left of the party and their schemes of construction. Yet from the start, Speaker Brand noted that it was 'a difficult team to drive'. Morley remarked that the Cabinet was a 'coalition of that vexatious kind where those who happened not to agree sometimes seemed to be almost as well pleased with contention as with harmony'.

Given this lack of tight control by the Prime Minister, it was all too easy, indeed in some cases necessary, for ministers to go their own way. Chamberlain did, and in so doing, was more than willing to use his press contacts to publicise his views rather than those of the government as a whole. The *Birmingham Daily Post* and other papers were pleased to receive articles, often unsigned, from him and this kind of activity often irritated his Whig colleagues.

This independent attitude gave him an obvious chance to speak and act as the main voice of popular Radical opinion. Though he resigned the Presidency of the NLF on entering the Cabinet, it was still much under his influence, and his power-base in the country was substantial.

Yet despite the considerable scope for individual action that Gladstone allowed, Chamberlain's strength within the Cabinet was not as great as he would have wished. His influence was limited by the distrust which many of his more experienced colleagues felt towards him. He and Dilke, a junior minister, often needed the support of these colleagues if they were to gain concessions, but it was often not provided. As Gladstone lacked sympathy towards him, Chamberlain found that achieving ministerial status did not mean acquiring power to shape the policy of the Cabinet.

Departmental Activity

His department did not attract much interest in political circles, but he quickly set about mastering its complexities. It had wide-ranging duties and there was scope for legislative action even though in the early years there would be little parliamentary time available for his measures. He came to recognise that changes made were likely to be useful rather than far-reaching, for as he explained to Morley in 1883: 'It is no use trying to elevate Bankruptcy and Patents into a new dispensation'. Such topics were, however, within his range of responsibility, and they featured in his reforming work.

In the early years of the Ministry, the lack of parliamentary time meant that there was little scope for legislation from his Department. In the first session, he was responsible for a limited measure which dealt with compensation for industrial accidents, the Employers Liability Act. In 1882, he took up Samuel Plimsoll's campaign on behalf of sailors and his Seamen's Wages Act secured an improved system of payment. A Grain Cargoes Act also provided for the safer stowing of cargoes. In that same year, his bill to allow local authorities to establish electricity supplies, either by themselves or through private companies was passed.

There was more room in the parliamentary programme in 1883 for other changes which Chamberlain wished to effect. His Patents Act and the

Bankruptcy Act were significant commercial measures, relatively uncontentious but useful. Yet the overall impact of such legislative measures was limited and they hardly amounted to the sort of programme of action that Chamberlain favoured.

Neither did his assault on the shipowners produce concrete achievement. His attempt to ensure greater safety at sea aroused furious opposition from the shipping magnates, many of whom were Liberals. The Government backed down and dropped the bill and Chamberlain had to be dissuaded from resigning over this.

He was also involved in commercial negotiations with France aimed at forcing that country to remove its protectionist tariffs against British goods. If anything, his desire for retaliatory measures was stronger than that of Dilke who handled much of the treaty-making. However, in August 1881, he argued against any general alteration to free trade policies because increasing tariffs on imported goods might lead to more expensive food. He was prepared to consider reciprocity agreements and even talked, in the early 1880s, of a British Zollverein, or customs union, with discriminatory duties against goods from outside the Empire. Ever a practical man of business, he was prepared to think critically about, rather than accept blindly, the benefits or otherwise of complete free trade.

He also took part in discussions over the merits of a Channel Tunnel, a project then being proposed. He inspected the preliminary digging in Dover, but was unimpressed by the venture and favoured giving no encouragement to its supporters.

Overall, Chamberlain's legislative record was a disappointment. He had been used to seeing his ideas carried out, but found that running a government department was not like galvanising a town's administration into action. Even most of his regulatory changes were already under discussion among interested parties and owed little to his personal initiative. His interest in the conditions of sailors showed his willingness to tackle entrenched interests, but his insensitive attacks on the owners had ruined any chance of getting a measure on the statute-book.

ATTITUDES TO COLONIAL POLICY

Chamberlain's involvement in national politics amounted to considerably more than his contribution as President of the Board of Trade. As an eloquent advocate of the Radical cause, he was interested in all the Government's work. In fact, most of his correspondence with Gladstone was on non-departmental matters. He could never be an inactive member of the Cabinet, and was pleased to have the scope to press his ideas in Downing Street and to a wider audience.

The Administration was not lacking in incident and drama. Overshadowed by events in Ireland, it ran into several other problems, especially abroad.

At the beginning of the Ministry, Chamberlain accepted that the annexation of the Transvaal would not be permanent and that the Boers would get their independence. After the defeat of the British forces at Majuba in 1881, some sought revenge but he accepted the restoration of independence. He expressed the hope that the Boer settlers and the Bantus, the native inhabitants, could live together with the latter being fairly treated. At this stage, no British economic or strategic interests were involved in South Africa, for this was before the discovery of gold in Witswatersrand.

Egypt was a difficult matter because the Suez Canal was now the main shipping route between Britain, India and the Far East. When a revolt broke out against the Khedive, a puppet ruler whom Britain and France had installed in the late 1870s, there was a clear threat to European control. Chamberlain had at first been dubious about plans to restore the Khedive's waning authority, but after riots in Alexandria in 1882, he became more bellicose in his attitude. Whereas Gladstone and some other Ministers intervened reluctantly, Chamberlain was, according to Granville, 'almost the greatest Jingo' on the issue. As British patriots clamoured for action, Chamberlain was prominent in arguing strongly for the bombardment of Alexandria.

To many other Radicals, the resulting British invasion was basically to protect British shareholders in the Suez Canal Company. Indeed, seeing Gladstone's action as 'worse than anything perpetrated by Dizzy', John Bright, the veteran Radical resigned from the Cabinet in protest. However, Chamberlain saw the matter as one of securing British interests and carrying out duties. He wanted to end the revolt and, by bringing about peace, to safeguard the Suez Canal route to India. He also stressed the importance of a Liberal Government seeking to develop representative institutions in Egypt, but hoped that evacuation of the area would be possible within a year or two – a hope that was not to be realised for seventy years.

Over Sudan and the revolt of a Muslim fanatic known as the Mahdi,

Chamberlain took a similarly strong line. He much disapproved of the 'new messiah' who had launched a revolt against brutal and inefficient Egyptian rule. The Khedive sent forces, commanded by a British officer, to crush the revolt; when that army was routed by the Mahdi in November 1883, Chamberlain saw it as a serious blow to British prestige.

There was widespread support for action, and Chamberlain shared such feelings. He backed Gladstone's decision to send General Gordon to the region; however, whereas Gladstone wanted Gordon to go in a purely advisory capacity, others, including Chamberlain, felt that he should have wider powers.

The General was a fearless evangelical Christian who wished to defeat the Mahdi and restore civilisation to the area. He exceeded his limited, but vague, instructions and as the forces of the Mahdi moved closer to Khartoum, his life was in danger. Gladstone initially delayed sending an expeditionary force to rescue him and finally did so only under intense Cabinet pressure; Chamberlain fully supported sending these relief troops. Unfortunately, they arrived too late, for Gordon was murdered in January 1885. The death of a popular hero was a damaging blow to the Ministry, and Chamberlain was appalled. He felt that Khartoum should be recaptured both to establish British control and defeat the Mahdi. However, Gladstone's view prevailed and for the time being Britain took no further action in the Sudan.

The events in Egypt and the Sudan show the extent of Chamberlain's developing Radical Imperialism. Committed to far-reaching reform at home, he combined this, unusually, with support for Britain's global interests and responsibilities in the same way as his friend Dilke was able to do.

THE CLASH WITH THE HOUSE OF LORDS

His Radical challenge reached its peak in 1884-6, with savage attacks on those bastions of privilege which blocked the way to wholesale reform. He was much involved in the discussions on the Franchise Bill designed to extend the vote to agricultural workers, a measure which aroused strong opposition from Tory peers. Faced with their obstruction, Chamberlain threw himself into a vigorous campaign against the Upper House. He denounced the 'arrogant and monstrous pretensions' of its members, and delighted his followers by his uncompromising attitude:

> We grudge the Lords nothing that rightly belongs to them . . . but when they claim to dictate the laws which we shall make, the way in which we shall govern ourselves – to spoil, delay, even reject measures demanded by the popular voice, passed after due discussion by a majority of the people's House, and receiving the sanction and confirmation of popular assemblies such as this – it is a claim contrary to reason, opposed to justice, and which we shall resist to the death.

There were angry scenes at many of his meetings, as he whipped up popular feeling. His attacks on Lord Salisbury as the representative of 'the class who toil not neither do they spin' became ever more forthright. He spoke of moving on to reform or even abolition of the House of Lords, but eventually a compromise was reached on the franchise Bill; the extension of the vote was balanced by a redistribution of seats.

Though it passed this Third Reform Act, the Administration's record failed to live up to the high expectations which many had of it in 1880. As it was drawing to a close, Chamberlain became increasingly restless, frustrated at the lack of a reforming programme. He would have liked the opportunity to leave the Ministry on an issue of principle, so that he could have taken the struggle to the constituencies where he had popular support. Eventually, disputes over the scheme for Irish self-government brought things to a head. When Gladstone was unwilling to back him against Cabinet objections, he and Dilke resigned shortly before the Government was brought down by a defeat in the Commons.

THE RADICAL CHALLENGE 1885-86

Towards the end of Gladstone's Ministry, Chamberlain's ideas were set out in the *Fortnightly Review*. Some articles were actually written by his supporters, John Morley and Jesse Collings, while others he wrote himself. In 1884-5, he launched an aggressive Radical campaign around the country, popularising some of the themes which had surfaced in press features and in meetings with friends. The speeches were very effective, and crowds flocked to hear his attacks on 'selfish wealth' and privilege.

In January 1885, the rich were alarmed when he outlined his theory of 'ransom'. This stressed that 'society owes a compensation to the poorer classes of this country, that it ought to recognize that claim and pay it'. The poor should be rewarded for meekly accepting that others owned much more than they did.

Ransom! Such a menacing term shocked both Liberals and Tories. Yet Chamberlain's objective was to stave off social revolution by urging the privileged to accept heavier taxation, the proceeds of which would go to help the less well off. Only by such measures could the rumblings of socialism be contained.

Prudently, he soon replaced the word 'ransom' with a more soothing one, 'insurance'. People could more easily understand this idea; if the rich paid their premiums by granting reform, their position in society would be safeguarded. By so doing, the owners of wealth and influence would be putting their rights of property 'on the only firm and defensible basis'.

In July 1885, soon after the fall of the Gladstone Government, he published a booklet, *The Radical Programme*, the first campaigning handbook of its kind in British politics. It included many of the ideas which he had put forward in recent months, and was intended to win over the support of the newly enfranchised voters in the countryside.

Shortly afterwards, his campaign moved into a higher gear, and he stepped up his speechmaking activities. His platform style was at its best, and the forcefulness of his language ensured that his attacks made the headlines. He denounced the House of Lords as 'the obsequious handmaid of the Tory Party', and vigorously criticised some of his Liberal colleagues for being timid and docile. It was stirring stuff, and the crowds loved it. On one occasion, he was hailed as 'Your coming Prime Minister', and a contemporary noted that, 'if audiences cheered Mr Gladstone's name for two minutes, they cheered Chamberlain's for five'.

Two future leaders were impressed. The young Ramsay MacDonald, who became the first Labour Prime Minister in 1924, was thrilled by the boldness of the speeches, and Lloyd George, the last Liberal PM, saw Chamberlain as his Radical hero; in comparison to his colleagues, he seemed so fearless and so positive. There was something exciting in what he offered, whereas their contributions seemed dull and grey.

As he thrilled his admirers, so he outraged his opponents. One Tory victim of his attacks, Lord Iddesleigh, saw him as like 'Jack Cade', who had led a rebellion in Kent against Henry VI. Lord Salisbury took up the theme by likening him to a 'Sicilian bandit', and others also viewed him as some kind of highwayman.

The fury extended to Whigs as well as to his political enemies, and several attacked him vigorously. Hartington had just reason to feel affronted, for Chamberlain's comparison of him to Rip Van Winkle was hardly a flattering one. Others found it extraordinary that a relatively junior minister of the last Cabinet should launch such assaults and make policy statements without first clearing them with the party leadership. But they also envied his flair for self-publicity!

It was one of those Whig colleagues, George Goschen, who coined the phrase the 'Unauthorised Programme', in an attempt to distance the programme from the official one put forward by Gladstone to his Midlothian electors (See pages 71f). In as much as the term implies a definite set of proposals it is misleading because in 1884-5 Chamberlain flirted with a whole range of ideas. Some were less often mentioned as time went by and others were in the Gladstone programme anyway. The more extreme policies in the handbook were scaled down as the election approached.

However, a few key themes repeatedly emerged. As he toured Scotland in the autumn, it was obvious that the slogan 'three acres and a cow' was a popular one, and so he began to emphasise those policies likely to appeal to the farm labourers. They were especially keen on his suggestion that local authorities should provide allotments and smallholdings for their benefit.

He also stressed his proposals on free elementary education, a graduated property tax and local government reform. Other ideas aired in the previous year, such as triennial parliaments, payment of MPs and manhood suffrage, were spoken of less often. When he realised that his plan for National Councils in England, Scotland, Wales and Ireland was not a vote-winner, that too was dropped from his campaign.

In this Unauthorised Programme, Chamberlain offered a typical Radical diagnosis of the country's problems. He recognised the great imbalance in the distribution of wealth, seeing 'excessive inequality' as a great evil. He emphasised that:

> It is not our duty, it is not our wish, to pull down and abase the rich, although I do not think that the excessive aggregation of wealth in a few hands is any advantage to anybody. But our object is to elevate the poor, to raise the general condition of the people . . .

He did not mind if the label 'Socialist' was applied to his proposals, for

> the greater part of municipal work is Socialism, and every kindly act of legislation by which the community has sought to discharge

a note on . . .

LIBERAL POLICIES IN 1885

Joseph Chamberlain

Title of Programme	The Unauthorised Programme
Circumstances of Delivery	Past articles put together in *The Radical Programme*, published in July; then speech-making.
Consultation	No discussion with any senior party figures, hence the title. Very much a personal programme.
Content	• Reform of House of Lords • Triennial Parliaments • Payment of MPs, Manhood Suffrage • Disestablishment of State Church • Democratic Local Govt. for counties • National Councils for Scotland, Wales and Ireland • Free elementary education • Graduated tax on property • Land reform to help agricultural labourers
Tone	The language used was inflammatory; it sounded more extreme than the content justified.
Reactions	Many Liberals, especially the Whigs, found its bellicose language most unattractive, and Gladstone was provoked to say that 'Chamberlain's socialism repels me'. Yet, though bold, the proposals were hardly revolutionary.

William Gladstone

Title of Programme	Manifesto (to Midlothian voters).
Circumstances of Delivery	Was playing a waiting game, and so issued just this statement as a political minimum.
Consultation	A personal creation, shown to very few; approved of by most of the ex-Cabinet members who saw it.
Content	Possibility of changes re Lords and in relations of Church and State; vague references to taxation 'during life and upon death'. Plus: • Reform of Commons Procedure • Local Government reform • Modest changes in land registration • Attempts to boost voter registration • No commitment on Ireland
Tone	Non-committal and lack-lustre.
Reactions	'A poor affair . . . a slap in the face to us', to Chamberlain; other Liberals were more contented.

its responsibilities and its obligations to the poor is Socialism and is none the worse for that.

He distinguished his position from that of Marxists, even though his opponents often branded him as a dangerous agitator with extreme left-wing beliefs:

Considering the difference in the character and capacity of men, I do not believe that there can ever be an absolute equality of conditions, and I think that nothing would be more undesirable than that we should remove the stimulus to industry and thrift and exertion . . . I am opposed to confiscation in every shape or form . . .

GLADSTONE AND THE ELECTION OF NOVEMBER 1885

Chamberlain's conduct in the pre-election period did not impress Gladstone. His very personal remarks made it hard for the leader to prevent a major rift in the party; in particular, Gladstone had to smooth relations with Hartington. Chamberlain's remarks on Ireland also made contacts with the Irish leader Charles Stewart Parnell more difficult.

Gladstone resented Chamberlain's lack of consultation, and was anyway unenthusiastic about 'programmatic politics', manifestoes which committed the party to specific future actions. The leader preferred to campaign on great and general causes, and not to make definite promises like the abolition of school fees or the compulsory purchase of land for the creation of allotments. He was, however, coming round to accepting the idea of graduated taxation, preferring this to the contemporary emphasis on indirect taxes.

Considering the problems which Chamberlain's forthright sallies caused the leader, relations between the two were not as bad as might have been expected. Gladstone neither liked the tone nor the content of some of Chamberlain's observations, and regarded him as a careerist. Chamberlain often felt frustrated by Gladstone's leadership, yet in the last few weeks before the election Chamberlain spoke warmly of him in public. He wanted to make sure that, if the Liberals won, Gladstone would give him an important post in the government.

In October 1885, Chamberlain visited Gladstone at Hawarden and, though the atmosphere was rather formal, it was nonetheless friendly. Gladstone did not commit himself to Chamberlain's proposals, telling him that 'Irish questions might elbow out all other things'. He anticipated that Ireland could suddenly erupt on the political scene, and so preferred to wait and then react to events when they occurred.

In the November election, the Liberal Party fared well in the rural areas, suggesting that the importance attached to the farm labourer's vote was not misplaced. As Chamberlain put it, 'the cow has been very well'. This measure of success put the Conservatives in a minority in the English counties for the first time with only 105 out of 239 seats. Overall, there was a deadlock; the Liberals had 335 seats against 249 for the Conservatives, so that the 86 Irish Nationalists held the balance exactly.

The Gladstone family took an unfavourable view of Chamberlain's role in the election; in some areas, they believed him to have been an electoral liability. Certainly, Gladstone was not willing to have party strategy taken over by his Radical challenger!

Ireland was likely to be the big issue in the coming months, and Gladstone had not yet declared his views on what steps should be taken. As it could well lead to political controversy, he hoped that Salisbury would remain as Prime Minister, and be the one to deal with its immediate problems.

Before we examine Irish events, however, there was a personal issue which engaged some of Chamberlain's attention, and which cast doubt upon his loyalty in matters of friendship.

THE DILKE CASE

As we have seen, Sir Charles Dilke was another prominent Radical and potential party leader. Whilst he never had anything like Chamberlain's support in the country at large, his ability and industry, combined with his aristocratic background, made him a likely successor when Gladstone retired. He and Chamberlain had been close colleagues in the previous Liberal Government. They had used each other's rooms at Westminster, and regularly confided in each other on matters relating to the party, its leadership and future prospects.

But in late 1885 and early 1886, an eventful time in English politics, Dilke had other preoccupations. He was involved in a divorce case which shocked Victorian society and destroyed his chance of securing high office. The case, in which he was named as a co-respondent, Crawford v Crawford and Dilke, reached the courts in February 1886.

As the evidence was unearthed in the trial, the attractive and young Mrs Crawford admitted that she and Dilke were lovers. More shockingly, some of their pastimes were alleged to involve frolics with a pretty servant with whom they shared the same bed. Such alleged activities, whilst perhaps a tribute to Dilke's virility, did nothing for his political reputation!

In the event, though Crawford got his divorce, the allegations against Dilke were not substantiated. The trouble was that the mud stuck and he was widely seen as a philanderer with a past, which almost ensured that Gladstone would not restore him to government office. In an attempt to clear his name of the charge, Dilke had the case reopened. The jury again believed Mr Crawford's account of Dilke's involvement, so that the effort failed, and his career was in ruins.

The House of Commons Lobby in 1886, as captured by Vanity Fair. Joseph Chamberlain is in the centre of the group standing next to the Irish leader Parnell (with the long beard) and opposite Gladstone (with the grey hair)

There were unresolved mysteries about the case. The honesty of Mrs Crawford was always open to doubt, as her accounts proved to be unreliable and inconsistent. They were still acutely damaging to Dilke.

Chamberlain's role in the events is difficult to ascertain. At times, he seemed to be recommending actions which ensured maximum publicity for the affair. For instance, he was keen to find Fanny, the serving-girl, to get her to testify at the trial. But, as she was thought to be an unreliable witness, her evidence could well have strengthened the case against Dilke rather than helped in his defence.

Mrs Crawford also visited Chamberlain shortly before her confession of adultery. When later tackled about the meeting, Chamberlain offered no explanation as to its purpose. As he always claimed that he did not know her, her arrival at that time is very surprising. As a result of this unexplained incident, there was always a suspicion that Chamberlain was involved in his friend's downfall. As an ambitious politician, it was argued, he stood to gain if Dilke were removed from the race for the leadership of the Liberal Party.

Yet Dilke, who always felt hurt if there seemed to be any coolness in their relations, did not believe that Chamberlain acted disloyally, and their friendship continued. Dilke's support for the Home Rule Bill in 1886 was more likely to have been the cause of any temporary rupture in their good relations.

Ultimately, whether he behaved treacherously or not, Chamberlain did not benefit from Dilke's downfall by gaining the leadership. However, at the time when Gladstone was about to form his third administration in January 1886, a serious rival had been discredited and removed from the scene.

1886 was to be a decisive year in Chamberlain's career, for Gladstone's Irish policy was to bring about his departure from the Liberal Party. As such, it marks the end of the effective Radical phase of his career.

timeline	1876	Elected MP
	1877	Formation of National Liberal Federation
	1880	Appointed as President of the Board of Trade
	1884	Struggle for Third Reform Act
	1885 July	'The Radical Programme' published
	November	General Election stalemate
	1886	President of the Local Government Board

Points to consider

1) In the years 1876-80, how did he seek to broaden the basis of his Radical appeal? What sort of causes did he take up?

2) Particularly as a Radical minister, he was unpopular with his colleagues. Why did they find him so difficult to work with?

3) Why was his performance in office not more productive of Radical reform?

4) Compare his attitude to the House of Lords in his early and later career. Why do you think his position changed? (See also Chapter 2)

5) Was his Unauthorised Programme really a fundamental attack on the existing social or economic system, or was he really concerned to shore the system up and make it more defensible?

6) He was a Radical but not a Marxist. Why did he disapprove of Marxism?

7) Does the Dilke affair tell us anything significant about Chamberlain's personality? Why was it relevant to the development of his career?

8) What held the Gladstonian Liberal Party together in these years?

CHAMBERLAIN, GLADSTONE AND IRELAND

In the nineteenth century, the Irish Question had a profound effect on the fortunes of several governments and the careers of many politicians. Gladstone was genuinely interested in the problems of Ireland, and resolving them became a personal mission. Although Chamberlain was never so committed, he similarly wished to produce a just settlement. But the differences in their attitudes to Ireland were to assume historic importance, and affected not just their own careers but the fate of the Liberal Party.

IRISH EVENTS 1880-85

Gladstone became Prime Minister at a time when there was much disorder in Ireland. He hoped to reduce the unrest by redressing grievances; his Land Act of 1881 responded to the problems by granting the so-called Three Fs – Fair Rents, Free Sale and Fixity of Tenure. Chamberlain fully supported the Land Act, describing it as 'our message of peace to the Irish people'. His hope was that such a generous gesture might destroy the impetus of the Irish campaign for Home Rule.

It soon became apparent that such agrarian reform would not alone pacify Ireland. Irish leaders saw it as a concession granted in response to their campaign of violence and disorder. From this judgement, they concluded that the greater the pressure they applied, the more the concessions they could secure.

In the following years, the Government's policy alternated between kicks and kindness, coercion and measures of conciliation. Faced with a further outbreak of terrorism, Gladstone reluctantly came to the view held by many of his colleagues that it was necessary to send Parnell, the Irish leader, to prison.

Chamberlain had opposed any coercive bill prior to the passage of the 1881 reform. A year earlier, he had explained that:

> Redress of acknowledged grievances should precede, or at least accompany, the suspension of the safeguards of liberty. The widespread disaffection of the Irish people grows out of causes of just complaint and it is to try to crush the one without first enquiring into and dealing with the other.

Once the Land Act was passed, it was reasonable to take a stronger line. In his view, anyone who was out to wreck it was an extremist, and, like Gladstone, he wanted to see a more moderate leadership emerge than that of Parnell. Accordingly, he supported his internment at Kilmainham; 'For my part, I hate coercion. I hate the name. I hate the thing . . . But I hate disorder more.' His attitude was hardening, and if it had to be a strong line, then 'coercion with a silk glove would be ridiculous'.

Gladstone knew that suppression was no answer and came to realise that it only created increased support for Parnell in Ireland. An opportunity to end the detention came when Parnell was temporarily released to visit a dying relative. The MP for County Clare, Captain O'Shea, wrote to Gladstone and Chamberlain suggesting negotiations, and Chamberlain and Captain O'Shea were the key figures in the events leading up to the Kilmainham Treaty of April 1882.

O'Shea's position was an interesting one. His wife was Parnell's mistress, and she had already borne Parnell's child. The O'Sheas lived apart, but the husband knew of the relationship. He knew that scandal would mean political death for Parnell, and was able to put pressure on Parnell to advance his own career interests. By assisting him in 1882, he felt he would deserve a favourable response.

Under the terms of the Treaty, Parnell and his colleagues were to use their influence to moderate the outrages and restore order in Ireland, and the Gladstone Government agreed to meet the debts of 100,000 Irish tenants who owed arrears of rent. Here also was a chance for a normalisation of relations between England and Ireland, for the Cabinet had become convinced that Parnell was no longer a threat to public order. Chamberlain felt that there was perhaps a real chance of reconciliation and reform.

However, within a very short time, any benefits which might have come from the agreement were shattered by the Phoenix Park murders. A terrorist group, the Invincibles, brutally murdered the new Chief Secretary, Cavendish, and the Permanent Under-Secretary, at Dublin Castle, using long surgical knives. Inevitably, there followed a demand for stiffer repressive measures which were introduced. A not-very-generous Arrears Act was also passed but this did not modify the less conciliatory atmosphere.

The impact of the assassinations on British opinion was considerable for they appeared to confirm a widely held suspicion that the Irish were at best irresponsible, unfit to govern themselves, while at worst they were bloodthirsty cut-throats. Parnell was shattered, and Gladstone and Chamberlain, the most reform-minded members of the Government, saw that there was little hope of further ameliorative measures.

Agrarian outrages gradually declined and for the rest of the Ministry the Irish MPs adopted a lower profile than before. The attention of ministers was diverted into other areas of policy, both at home and abroad. Chamberlain remained interested in Ireland, and continued to have serious doubts about the use of force to quell discontent. He still recognised the need for reform, and protested when his proposals for public works to ease conditions fell on deaf ears.

He was radical in his social policy towards Ireland. He believed that a policy of reform should tackle legitimate grievances and lessen the hardships the Irish endured. Such a policy he felt might also weaken the influence of the extremists who thrived on the discontent. Thus, rather than merely crushing disorders, he believed that it was 'the better and higher work of the Liberals to find out the cause of disaffection and to remove it'. But Parnell, for his part, could never understand how a person who was so forward-looking and constructive in social policy could at the same time be unwilling to approve Home Rule, a major change in the constitutional relationship of England to Ireland.

ATTITUDES TO HOME RULE
—

Chamberlain had already made his view clear on Home Rule in 1874:

> If Mr. Butt . . . (the leader of the Home Rule Party) . . . may be
> considered as a true exponent of the views of the Home Rulers, I
> am in favour of the system he advocates, and I believe also that the

a note on . . .

HOME RULE

DEFINITION

Home Rule means limited autonomy or self-government, and it was the goal of the Irish Nationalists to achieve self-government over Ireland's domestic affairs. They objected to the Act of Union (1800) between England and Ireland, and believed that Ireland could govern itself better than England could. Since its application in Ireland, the term has been more widely used to refer to any claim for partial autonomy by a minority group.

THE CAMPAIGN FOR HOME RULE

The 'Home Government Association' was formed in Dublin in 1870 by Isaac Butt, who is widely credited with inventing the term. He sat as a Home Ruler at Westminster from 1871-9, and tried to convert English opinion by reasoned argument. The Association then became known as the Home Rule League in 1873, and by the late 70s its members were more militant. They deliberately obstructed proceedings in the House of Commons to force other politicians to pay attention to their cause. In 1878, Butt was replaced by the more aggressive Charles Stewart Parnell who supported such tactics.

THE LIBERALS AND HOME RULE

In the 19th century, the Liberals were traditionally supportive of peoples overseas struggling for their freedom, and Gladstone applied this approach to the Irish situation. He moved away from pacification, because he came to see that reform of conditions was not enough; he recognised that the Irish were a nation who wanted a say in the way they were governed. Persuading his party and the public to accept Home Rule would be difficult, especially after the feelings of revulsion aroused by the Phoenix Park murders.

FIRST HOME RULE BILL, 1886

Gladstone proposed that Ireland should be given a Parliament and an executive in Dublin, whilst Britain would retain control of several important 'reserved subjects'. Irish representation at Westminster was to be ended, so that in future there would be no Irish MPs to cause obstruction or hold the balance of power between the parties. The bill was defeated by 30 votes.

SECOND HOME RULE BILL 1893

This modified the 1886 measure; it differed mainly in that it allowed for continued Irish representation at Westminster. As in the earlier version, no special protection was offered for the Protestants in the north, who feared that they would be submerged in a Catholic Parliament. This time, there was a heavy defeat in the Lords.

THIRD HOME RULE BILL 1912-14

Again, there was to be Irish representation at Westminster to secure the supremacy of the Imperial Parliament; the Irish were to have more power over their internal affairs. During the passage of this bill, opposition in Ulster became intense, and the country lurched towards civil war. It became law in the summer of 1914, but the implementation of the statute was postponed because of the war.

Opponents of Home Rule like Chamberlain often claimed that it would be the first stage towards Irish independence and, therefore, the break-up of the United Kingdom. He spoke of Home Rulers and Separatists in the same breath, though Gladstone never viewed Home Rule in this way. To him, it represented a chance to resolve the Irish problem through peaceful means, and to do so in a way which would not destroy the Union of England and Ireland. The 'reserved subjects' were significant ones, so that the reality of the Home Rule he proposed was far short of independence.

extension of the system of local government would be of the greatest advantage to England and Ireland. It is only candid and fair to add that I am not in favour of any system which would go further than this, and which would separate the Imperial relation between the two countries.

His thinking about the relationship between England and Ireland began to develop in 1884, and he produced a variety of proposals ranging from local government reform to a more substantial recasting of the bonds between the two countries. He could accept the need to satisfy the legitimate desire of the Irish for a say in their own government, 'for a local control of purely domestic affairs'. He was prepared for this to be a significant measure of devolution, the most extensive measure of self-government consistent with the overall supremacy of the United Kingdom Parliament at Westminster. He would not, however:

consent to regard Ireland as a separate people with the inherent rights of an absolutely independent community. I should not do this in the case of Scotland, or of Wales, or, to take more extreme instances, of Sussex or of London. In every case, the rights of country or district must be subordinated to the rights of the whole community of which it only forms a portion. Ireland, by its geographical position, and by its history, is a part of the United Kingdom.

He proposed a scheme for an 'Irish (or 'Central') Board' to deal with such questions as education, land and other matters which could be handled locally. Such a Board might be directly elected, or could comprise delegates from the new system of county councils which he also favoured. The second Gladstone Government rejected this idea shortly before it fell.

In the summer and autumn of 1885, the scheme was developed in the Unauthorised Programme into a proposal for local legislatures for England, Scotland, Wales and Ireland, the new bodies to be known as 'National Councils'. These would handle domestic matters, whilst allowing the integrity of the United Kingdom to be maintained via continued representation of the four countries at Westminster. Confusingly, the label 'Home-Rule-All-Round' was often applied to such initiatives.

Some form of federal solution appealed to Chamberlain's sense of order – generous devolution, involving equal treatment for all of the home countries. To him, this would cater for Irish aspirations, but do so within the context of the United Kingdom.

The core of the Parnell case, however, was that the Irish Question was a national issue which could only be dealt with by a bolder settlement. He suspected that Chamberlain's proposal was designed to shelve any plan for Home Rule which involved the creation of an Irish Parliament. Though at the time not a professed separatist, Parnell could not accept that it was possible to fix the boundaries of a nation; there might come a time when Ireland would demand its independence, and he would support that wish. Chamberlain, from his earliest involvement, was clear that national independence must never be conceded to Ireland.

By 1885, Gladstone had come to realise that tackling economic and religious problems was not by itself enough to placate the Irish, who wanted their own Parliament. At some point in his second Ministry, his thinking moved away from pacification to granting some form of self-government. The removal of individual grievances was important and did something to remove the injustices of English rule. However, it was the existence of English rule itself that was at the heart of the matter, so that no solution would be successful that did not involve a measure of devolution.

Significantly, Gladstone had never made a speech against Home Rule since 1881, and though he had spoken of the difficulties involved in separating Irish and Imperial affairs, he was prepared to give them sympathetic consideration. He was indirectly in touch with Parnell, through Mrs. O'Shea and his son, Herbert. It became clear that the Irish leader would accept nothing short of an Irish Parliament, separate from the British Parliament.

Whatever and whenever the exact circumstances of his conversion, Gladstone did not make his views on the desirability of Home Rule public in the early months after the fall of the government in June 1885. Chamberlain was, therefore, unaware of Gladstone's change of heart. He was, however, absolutely clear about his own position. He took the view that to concede such a measure would lead to a dissolution of the union of England and Ireland. Such a separation, he believed, would ultimately jeopardise the integrity not just of the United Kingdom but of the British Empire.

THE HAWARDEN KITE

Gladstone remained silent about his intentions concerning Home Rule, rather hoping that the Salisbury Government might be induced to take up the cause. There were precedents for the Tories pushing through controversial measures (most notably in 1846 over the Repeal of the Corn Laws) and a bipartisan approach would be much less damaging to his party. Whatever happened, however, as he kept his counsel, he did not want to allow any diminution in the Liberal commitment to Irish reform.

On 16 December, the 'Hawarden Kite' was flown. Herbert Gladstone conveyed his father's conversion to Home Rule to the press. This may have been an 'indiscretion', as Professor Mansergh suggests, or, more probably, he was floating an idea in a deliberate press leak, so that the Gladstone family could gauge reactions to the announcement. Whether Gladstone personally knew of Herbert's intervention is uncertain, but once his views had been made known, there was little point in stalling any longer by issuing a categorical denial.

When the story broke, the political situation was dramatically changed. As the Conservatives came out strongly against Home Rule, the Liberals became the party identified with it. Hartington let it be known that he was not prepared to support the new policy, and Chamberlain, Harcourt and Dilke met Gladstone on New Year's Day 1886, to find a way of stopping him in his tracks.

The attempt to block Gladstone failed, and he knew that Parnell could now be counted on to turn out the Tories and support a Liberal Government which offered the only hope of Home Rule for Ireland. On January 2, 1886, the Liberals put down an amendment to the Queen's Speech in the hope that a vote on it would bring about Salisbury's downfall. Rather than do so on the divisive Irish question, they opted for a Chamberlainite motion on the 'three acres and a cow' theme. It was moved by Jesse Collings, Chamberlain's lieutenant, now a fellow MP for Birmingham. The Government was defeated, having lost the support of Parnell and the Irish, and it accepted the amendment as a vote of 'no confidence' in the administration.

THE THIRD GLADSTONE GOVERNMENT, 1886, AND HOME RULE

In January 1886, Gladstone was excited to be back in office, though this time without the support of some of his old colleagues, including Bright and Hartington. In the period of Cabinet construction, Chamberlain was initially offered the post of First Lord of the Admiralty which was hardly attuned to his interests. He turned it down and expressed his preference for the office of Colonial Secretary, provoking Gladstone to respond with some horror; 'Oh, a Secretary of State'! Garvin records that the Prime Minister 'raised his head and dismissed tacitly without one further syllable of comment' Chamberlain's desire for a significant Department.

That refusal mortified Chamberlain because of its implied message, namely that he was not up to the job. It seemed as though Gladstone attached little importance to Chamberlain's support and ideas. Not surprisingly, he felt ill-used and undervalued. The Prime Minister intended the Colonial Office to be for a person of aristocratic connections, and instead he offered Chamberlain the relatively minor Presidency of the Local Government Board. If its status was lowly, it was at least a topic on which Chamberlain was well-informed from his personal experience in Birmingham.

Chamberlain was trapped in a difficult position. He had no obvious reason for refusing to serve; to do so would seem like personal pique. Yet he knew that Gladstone was likely to produce an Irish policy which he could not accept. His resignation at some point was highly probable, as Gladstone well understood. It would then be seen as though Chamberlain was the cause of any subsequent rift in the party.

Gladstone was tactless in his handling of Chamberlain at this time, and inflicted another wound. As his Parliamentary Secretary, Chamberlain secured the appointment of Jesse Collings but was exasperated when Gladstone tried to bring about a reduction in Collings' salary for reasons of economy. Collings was not the only junior member of the Government to be treated in this way, but to Chamberlain it seemed like a personal snub. Eventually, he managed to ensure that 'poor Collings' was not denied the whole of 'his scanty pittance'.

Further hurt and frustration followed, for having drawn up an unsolicited but comprehensive scheme of local government reform the new President found that his plans were not even discussed in Cabinet. At key points in the early weeks of the new Government, Gladstone's insensitive handling of Chamberlain provoked offence, and made it clear that he was unconcerned about retaining his services.

Within the Cabinet, Chamberlain was even more isolated than in 1880-85. His one-time confidant, Morley, had moved to support Home Rule, and, of course, Dilke was otherwise engaged. Yet, as the Ministry lacked a number of established figures, he was still the second most influential person in the Liberal Party.

He had taken office on the understanding that Gladstone was pledged to tackle the Irish question. From the start it was known that he was opposed to the idea of an Irish Parliament, but he undertook to give 'an unprejudiced consideration' to any new proposals. In return, he was promised a full Cabinet discussion of his own alternative suggestions which ranged over education and local government reform, but, above all, dealt with the land issue. Such a thorough examination never took place, for Gladstone did not put his memorandum on the agenda of a Cabinet session. As far as he was concerned, such policies were no substitute for Home Rule and would never placate Parnell and the Irish MPs.

When the first Home Rule Bill was produced on 26 March, 1886, Chamberlain resigned, much to Gladstone's satisfaction. The bill proposed a separate Parliament for Ireland with full powers over domestic affairs, though there were to be certain important exclusions, such as matters of peace and war, defence, foreign relations, international trade, customs and excise, and coinage. There were to be no Irish members in the House of Commons. Chamberlain felt that this was a sticking point, for such representation would have at least maintained the ultimate supremacy of the British Parliament. In addition, there would have been scope for creating a separate assembly for Ulster. Such changes would have turned the bill into something resembling his proposal of Home-Rule-All-Round.

In the debates which took place between April and early June, there followed one of the most memorable struggles in parliamentary history. Chamberlain spoke against the Government on the bill's First Reading, as he did on the Second one. In his speeches, he took up the question of Ulster, which Lord Randolph Churchill was exploiting to the full. The predominantly Protestant population there had no wish to be submerged in a largely Catholic Irish Parliament in which its interests would carry little weight. Chamberlain saw the importance of this emotional issue and recognised that it was the weakest point of the Government's position. He drove home the political advantage, remarking that:

> It is the difficulty, one of the great difficulties of this problem, that Ireland is not a homogeneous community, that it consists of two nations, that it is a nation which comprises two races and two religions.

Chamberlain's attack was effective, and when the division came at the end of the Second Reading, the bill was defeated by 343 to 313. Chamberlain and 92 other Liberals voted with the Conservative Opposition. Following such a setback, Gladstone called an election for July in which the Liberals received what he recognized as a 'real drubbing'.

WHY DID CHAMBERLAIN RESIGN?

Though he initially claimed that he was unhappy about Gladstone's land purchase scheme which was to accompany the main bill, there was a clear principle involved in his resignation. Chamberlain was opposed to an Irish Parliament which he felt would inevitably lead to separation. When he spoke of any scheme of devolution or Home Rule, he supported a system of government consistent with the preservation of a United Kingdom; as far as he was concerned, the Gladstonian scheme went far beyond this in that it weakened and thus threatened the union of England and Ireland.

He felt that, in the long run, the Bill would surely lead to the 'absolute national independence of Ireland', and the break-up of the United Kingdom. This would diminish Britain's strength and status, and that the 'country would sink to the rank of a third-rate power'. Such a view was an overstatement of what was on offer. There were enough exclusions in the Bill to ensure that Westminster's influence would prevail in vital areas, and Gladstone framed his measure in a way designed to meet Irish aspirations without jeopardising the links binding the two countries. It was, in that sense, a conservative solution; whether in the longer term it could have achieved this is, of course, open to question.

Chamberlain may have been resisting the Bill for the reason given, whatever the accuracy of his judgement. Yet was he not also using this issue as a means of breaking up the old Liberal Party? After all, a decade earlier he was seeking to refashion the Liberal cause, and in the meantime he had become more impatient with the leadership. Gladstone seemed to be a barrier to his plans for social reform, and now the preoccupation with Ireland prevented the party from pursuing radical initiatives.

However, a break-up hardly seemed in his interest, and resignation was unlikely to offer much scope for immediate political advancement. In some respects things looked more optimistic in the longer view. Gladstone could not go on forever, and Hartington and the Whigs were being frightened off by Gladstone's plans for Ireland.

If Gladstone succeeded in carrying Home Rule, then the divisive issue would have been out of the way and, his mission accomplished, the Prime Minister might have retired from the scene. If he failed, then someone known to have been cool towards the proposal might have been well placed to take over. (He was not to know that Gladstone would try again a few years later!).

He was undoubtedly ambitious, and for some historians this was the decisive consideration. O'Hegarty, in *Ireland under the Union*, finds it:

> impossible not to lean to the conclusion that the deciding factor in Chamberlain's career, the wrecking of Home Rule and the Liberal Party, was the belief that the summit of his political ambition was now within his grasp, were he but bold enough.

Considerations of principle and personal advantage were both probably involved in his decision to resign. Beyond such factors, there was the sad history of the relationship between the two men. Chamberlain knew that Gladstone had little respect for him and the attitudes which he represented, and may well have felt unable to take any more of the slights which the Prime Minister seemed intent on inflicting upon him.

CHAMBERLAIN, GLADSTONE AND THE DRAMA OF 1886; A REFLECTION

The relationship of Gladstone and his daring younger colleague, Chamberlain, throws revealing light on their respective characters. It is also significant as the antagonism between them had a tremendous impact on party politics in the late nineteenth century. Their dealings had never been easy, and by 1885 they were strained and uncertain. In the following months, the clash developed into one of the most passionate struggles in the history of modern parliamentary conflict.

Despite their contrasting personalities and outlook, these were two men who could have accomplished much together. Both had commanding and constructive gifts to offer. Their differing experience made them mutually complementary, for, as Hammond observed, Chamberlain lacked the European insight which lighted Gladstone's mind to the truth about Irish government, but possessed a zeal for action on social questions in which the Prime Minister lacked.

It is impossible to say whether, acting together, they could have secured Home Rule. They may have put through some measure of devolution. Certainly, with the departure of the Whig element, much could have been achieved in England and Ireland by cooperation. After all, in the run-up to the 1885 election, they had managed to reconcile their differences over the Unauthorised Programme.

However, cooperation was only possible during the brief periods when their interests brought them together, such as over the Bulgarian atrocities. There had never been any great sympathy between them; each could recognize the obvious qualities of the other, but the two men were diverse in mind, temperament and approach to policy issues. Gladstone believed in the 'politics of passion', absorbing himself in great moral crusades, whereas Chamberlain preferred constructive and practical schemes of radical reform.

Both were guilty of a lack of tact and understanding, but Gladstone, as party leader, must take a substantial share of the blame for this. He often showed the least generous side of his nature in his treatment of Chamberlain. On more than one occasion, he failed to make the best use of his ambition and his radicalism.

He could have offered Chamberlain a more senior post in 1880; there were opportunities to conciliate him in 1882, when a new Irish Secretary was needed, and again in 1886 when the new government was formed. However, Gladstone had two standards when judging men for public life, one for Whigs, another for Radicals, and they were weighted against the latter. By comparison, Disraeli had a gift for gathering young men about him even if they came from a dissimilar environment and had differing views.

If Gladstone had treated Chamberlain with more consideration, he may well have won his cooperation. He found it difficult to do this. He could never fully fathom the force and qualities of Chamberlain, and confessed to his friend, Lord Acton, that he found him unintelligible. According to Hammond, he failed to understand the character of most public men! In Chamberlain's case, the views expressed were often particularly incomprehensible, for as Gladstone wrote to Acton in 1885:

> The pet idea (of the Liberalism of today) is what they call constructionism . . . taking into the hands of the state the business of individual men. Both this Liberalism and Tory Democracy have done much to estrange me, and have done for many years.

He also disliked Chamberlain's demagogic style just as much as his Whig colleagues did. The experience of 1880–85 had revealed that Chamberlain was a man of independent speech who could outrage their sense of what was proper and respectful in a new minister. The use made by him and Dilke of their press friendships to advance their own ideas (particularly when they knew that they were not shared by their colleagues) was a further irritation, and Gladstone also had difficulties with the Queen on his account.

In many ways, therefore, Chamberlain came under suspicion as a man whose methods were unconventional, if not unscrupulous. Gladstone felt he could never trust him and, as proud man, he resented the ambitious self-seeking that his rival displayed. He was not prepared to look beyond the cocksure arrogance that Chamberlain showed, and consequently failed to appreciate the ability and skills that lay beneath the surface.

If Gladstone's distrust of Chamberlain and neglect of his reforming talents reveals him at his worst, then Chamberlain's attitude in 1886 is also open to criticism. J.W. Derry, in *The Radical Tradition*, has remarked that:

> Just as Gladstone's advocacy of Home Rule had failed because he did not understand Chamberlain, so Chamberlain's dreams of a revivified Liberal Party were dashed by his own inability to appreciate the intensity of Gladstone's devotion to Home Rule.

Chamberlain did not appreciate that, to the Prime Minister, Home Rule was his life's mission, from which he would never turn away.

His understanding of the Irish Question was also suspect. In February, he told Gladstone that if the issue was between 22 million and 4 million people, then he would not like to appease Parnell – with whom he was now on bad terms. He should have realised that his programme of Irish reform was not enough to capture the imagination of Ireland, and that its demands had to be met. He was as blind at this stage to Ireland's problems as Gladstone was on English social reform.

CHAMBERLAIN AND IRISH POLICY AFTER 1886

After 1886, as Chamberlain drifted towards the Conservatives, his attitude on Irish affairs remained much the same. He welcomed measures of agrarian reform passed by the second Salisbury Administration, and continued to oppose Home Rule strongly. His radicalism became less important to him than his desire to maintain the unity of the United Kingdom at all costs. In 1889, he outlined this thinking in Glasgow;

> In my opinion, every Liberal who places the Union first of all is bound to make some sacrifices for what will be his paramount object. He is bound to make some sacrifices of extremist views. He is bound to put aside for a time some of his cherished ambitions.

Above all, he believed in the union of England and Ireland, as part of a United Kingdom. Because of this, he could share a platform with the Conservative Prime Minister in Birmingham Town Hall in 1891, and propose a toast to the Unionist cause. He would work with anyone who shared his commitment. His importance as a Liberal Unionist was increased when he took over the leadership of the group on Hartington's succession to the House of Lords.

The Liberal Unionists helped to organise an Ulster Convention in June 1892, and this showed the strength of feeling of opinion there. Protestants were determined not to be a minority in a predominantly Catholic Irish Parliament, and Chamberlain began to reflect these concerns in a series of speeches. After the Liberal victory in the election of that year, he had good reason to give warnings over the renewed dangers of Home Rule – for Gladstone was again Prime Minister. This time, however, Parnell was no longer on the scene, for his career had been brought to a dramatic end.

CHAMBERLAIN AND PARNELL; THE O'SHEA DIVORCE CASE

Chamberlain had initially been impressed by Parnell, observing in him qualities not unlike some of his own. He had written of his industry, 'his unflinching determination in what he believes to be right – his courage, his coolness'. He came to dislike him intensely.

They took an entirely different attitude to the constitutional relations of England and Ireland. Chamberlain's mind was fertile in producing schemes of Irish government which Parnell regarded as at best a diversion from Home Rule. The Irish leader made little attempt to win him round, and Chamberlain found himself fiercely denounced in the nationalist press. In Parnell's own newspaper, United Ireland, he was described as 'a sort of shopkeeping Danton, probably the very best imitation a nation of shopkeepers could produce'. The phrase was deliberately offensive, suggesting that he lacked the qualities of a first-rate leader.

Such calculated abuse rankled Chamberlain who found Parnell politically and personally offensive. He also believed that the Parnellites were not representative of the Irish people. He always hoped that a less uncompromising figure might emerge to replaced him as leader. Then his plans for limited devolution might receive a more sympathetic response.

From an early stage, certainly by the time of the Kilmainham negotiations he knew of Parnell's adulterous relationship with Katherine O'Shea, certainly by the time of the Kilmainham negotiations. The relationship was useful to the Liberal Government in that messages could be conveyed through her to Parnell, just as Captain Willie O'Shea could be used as an intermediary in negotiations.

Parnell, the 'uncrowned King of Ireland', had been living with Mrs O'Shea, his 'Queenie', since 1881, though not continuously so until 1886. It was an affair of great passion, and one well-known in the political world. At first, the husband was unaware of his wife's liaison, but when it became obvious he chose to ignore it.

O'Shea and his wife had lived apart for many years, but they came together at weekends and outwardly seemed to be a happy couple. She enjoyed being the wife of an MP and hoped to see his career advance. He shared this ambition, and recognised that the Parnell association could do him some good, much as he despised her lover. The O'Sheas had another common bond. O'Shea was always short of money, and they were heavily dependent on her very old Aunt 'Ben', whose death was long-awaited. As long as she lingered, it was particularly necessary to maintain the image of domestic harmony and avoid a scandal.

O'Shea gained a few political benefits, for Parnell used him to convey information to Gladstone – via Joseph Chamberlain. Parnell even insisted that he be found a new constituency in 1886, after his defeat in the previous election. Yet however much he might benefit in this way, O'Shea's contempt for his party leader knew no bounds. When *The Times* published a number of articles in 1887 on 'Parnellism and Crime', he had high hopes that Parnell's career might be seriously damaged. The series did not arouse widespread interest until one particular letter was quoted. It showed that, though Parnell had publicly condemned the Phoenix Park murders, he had privately condoned them. The revelations caused a sensation, though Parnell immediately branded the document a forgery.

The Conservatives revelled in the disclosures and Chamberlain quickly exploited the issue, for he sensed an opportunity to discredit Parnell. This was despite the fact that in the immediate aftermath of the Phoenix Park murders, Parnell had come to see him 'white as a sheet, and completely demoralised', in fear of his life. Chamberlain urged that there should be a Special Committee of three judges to examine the whole affair and not the parliamentary Select Committee which the Liberals and the Irish MPs favoured. Parnell reluctantly agreed to defend himself before such a tribunal, and when Richard Pigott, an Irish journalist, confessed to forging the letter and other documents, Parnell's reputation in England and Ireland soared. However, the glory was to be short-lived.

O'Shea was by now desperate to see Parnell brought down, and Chamberlain was looking for another opportunity. He had persuaded O'Shea to resign his seat, and the Captain found himself without a career and without a wife. When Aunt 'Ben' finally died, O'Shea was to be bought off with £20,000, so that Katherine could finally be rid of him. But the will was contested by other relatives, and it looked likely to be deprived of his fortune as well. Financially disappointed, and with no chance of any further pickings from Parnell, he sued his wife for divorce, naming Parnell as co-respondent.

The exact role of Joseph Chamberlain in this complex saga is difficult to establish. It has been suggested that he persuaded O'Shea to bring the court action, and the allusion of Sir Alfred Robbins, a Birmingham journalist, to enquiries he received from a prominent Liberal Unionist is taken to refer to Chamberlain. The queries related to the likely effects of another Dilke-type scandal on the fortunes of Parnell, should O'Shea be willing to act against his wife.

There is no doubt that Chamberlain was looking to see Parnell fall from grace, and was willing to take steps to bring about his downfall. He had high hopes that the *Times'* accusations would ruin him, and when they failed to stick, Parnell's private life became a second line of attack. He had used O'Shea as a channel of communication, and had influence over him. He had persuaded him to testify in the Enquiry hearings and to resign his Galway seat, had lent him money, and had worked with him in 'digging up the dirt' on Parnell. It is reasonable, therefore, to surmise that he put O'Shea up to bringing the case.

The Captain certainly kept Chamberlain closely informed on the details of his divorce action. Many years later Austen and Neville Chamberlain speculated on their father's involvement. Austen recalled that O'Shea spent a night at Highbury shortly before the proceedings, but he did not know what was discussed; 'Evidently Father knew of the proceedings beforehand, but that does not prove he instigated them'.

Whether or not he was the inspiration for O'Shea's initial move for divorce, he was closely connected with the unsavoury subsequent attempt to halt Parnell's career in the trial. It says something of Chamberlain's reputation that there were so many rumours that he was somehow involved.

For his many critics, particularly in the Liberal and Irish parties, his conduct merely confirmed their view of him. They found it all too easy to believe that he would act unscrupulously to advance his own prospects or engineer an opponent's downfall especially after the Dilke case. After all, not many public figures have loomed in the shadows in two divorce cases in so short a time.

His wish to see Parnell's fall was granted. The divorce case was uncontested, and a decree nisi was granted to O'Shea. In Victorian times, divorce amounted to disgrace, and, though Parnell hoped to resist the mounting pressure, he was faced with a powerful combination of critics in the Liberal Party, amongst the Catholic clergy and from within the ranks of his own parliamentary group. Totally discredited, and with his support ebbing away, he died only four months after marriage to the woman for whom he had placed his career and cause in jeopardy.

THE CLASH OVER THE SECOND HOME RULE BILL

The clash between Gladstone and Chamberlain in the Home Rule debate was a very dramatic one, and ranged from moments of sharp antagonism to ones of great chivalry. In the months in which the bill occupied the House, the 83 year old Prime Minister fought day after day in the Chamber, and brilliantly steered it through its three Readings. Behind him, prominently positioned on the third bench, sat Chamberlain. Not yet 60, and looking considerably younger, he was a tenacious and trenchant critic. Gladstone told the Queen that he 'stood very decidedly first in ability among the opponents'.

At one point, after Chamberlain had mocked the Liberals for their 'slavish adulation' of Gladstone, the situation was so tense that there were actually scuffles on the floor of the House; words like 'Judas' were hurled at the younger adversary.

Yet there was also an occasion of some poignancy when Austen Chamberlain now an MP, made his maiden speech. Chamberlain could hardly conceal his emotion when Gladstone complimented him warmly, remarking that the intervention 'must have been dear and refreshing to a father's heart'.

On two occasions Joseph Chamberlain had been a key figure in the opposition to Home Rule, though on this second occasion it was the Duke of

Devonshire (formerly Lord Hartington) who also played a decisive part in its defeat through his attack in the House of Lords.

After this setback, and Gladstone's retirement in 1894, the Liberals could hardly disown their official policy of Home Rule, but, with Gladstone gone, the issue was kept in the background. By now, Chamberlain was clearly in the anti-Liberal camp. He remained a Liberal Unionist, rather than a Conservative, but on the question of the union of England and Ireland was at one with Salisbury. At a time of Imperial sentiment, when the British Empire was expanding overseas, there could in his view be no destruction of the integrity of the United Kingdom at home.

In 1895, he felt able to serve in a Conservative and Unionist Government. By using the term 'Unionist', to cover all those who shared his views on Ireland's status, he could retain his credibility and popular support, and yet work with the official Conservatives; in his own words:

> I am, and shall be in the future, proud to call myself a Unionist, and be satisfied with that title alone, believing it is a wider and nobler title than that either of Conservative or Liberal, since it includes them both – since it includes all men who are determined to maintain an undivided Empire, and who are ready to promote the welfare and the union not of one class but of all classes of the community.

By then, the political and social ties between Liberal Unionism and the Conservative Party were strong; they were to grow steadily closer in the coming years, and eventually lead to complete amalgamation.

timeline	1881		Land Act
	1882	April	Kilmainham Treaty
		May	Phoenix Park murders
	1885	Dec	Hawarden Kite; Gladstone's attitude leaked
	1886		New (Third) Gladstone Administration
		March	Resignation of Chamberlain
		June	Defeat of First Home Rule Bill
	1887	Feb	Failure of Round Table Conference
		March	'The Times' published 'Parnellism and Crime'
	1891		Death of Parnell
	1893	Sept	Second Home Rule Bill rejected in Lords

Points to consider

1) Was Chamberlain sympathetic to the Irish in his early approach to the handling of the Irish Question?
2) What similarities and differences were there in the attitudes of Gladstone and Chamberlain to Irish affairs?
3) What were Chamberlain's objections to Home Rule? How consistent was his thinking on the subject?
4) 'Parnell was at heart a separatist, Chamberlain an Imperialist'. Was the gulf so unbridgeable that no agreed solution to the Irish problem could ever have been reached?
5) 'There goes the man who killed Home Rule'. Did Chamberlain's opposition to Home Rule ruin its chances of being adopted?
6) Why do you think that Gladstone was unwilling to offer more attractive and influential Cabinet positions to Chamberlain?
7) To whom do you allocate the greater responsibility, Gladstone or Chamberlain, for the want of understanding between them?
8) What evidence is there that Chamberlain was keen to bring about the fall of Parnell?
9) Who actually understood the Irish Question more, Chamberlain or Gladstone?
10) Do you think that Home Rule could ever have solved the Irish Question?

7

THE EMPIRE

In 1895, Chamberlain was back in office, this time as a member of a mainly Conservative Cabinet. As Colonial Secretary, his new task presented another huge challenge, in a similar way that his mission to clear the Birmingham slums had done. He was to find that municipal problems were more easily remedied than were the worst problems of the Empire. There was such a diverse assortment of territories to administer. Chamberlain's responsibility was for everything other than that which came under the control of the Secretary of State for India.

There was some surprise that a politician of his eminence had wanted a post which had a relatively low standing in the hierarchy of government office. He was offered a free choice of Cabinet posts, and was encouraged to go to the Home Office or to the Exchequer, but he was in no doubt. The Colonial Secretaryship was the position he had really wanted in 1886, and which had provoked Gladstone's crushing response. Now, his wish was granted.

Chamberlain had been interested in the development and expansion of the Empire for several years, and, like his friend Dilke, had been a Radical Imperialist. With Home Rule off the immediate political agenda, he had begun to place more and more emphasis on the Imperial theme – his desire for the Colonial Office was a natural expression of his enthusiasm for the colonies. He took office in the hope of 'furthering closer union between them and the United Kingdom'. Apart from the chance to fulfil such a dream, the Empire offered other benefits.

From a personal standpoint it provided a field in which he could cooperate with the Tories. Whatever reservations some of them might have had about his Radical past, his robust support for Monarchy and Empire was bound to lessen their anxieties. Yet at the same time, he could still stay in touch with the rising generation of Liberal Imperialists or 'Limps', such as Roseberry, Asquith and Grey. Such men looked likely to feature prominently in the post-Gladstonian Liberal Party.

He knew that the Empire aroused much excitement at home because it reflected the rising spirit of patriotism. Many working men were inspired by thoughts of a wider role for Britain. Contemporary songs and hymns held out the prospect of a Greater Britain from which men and women went out to spread the benefits of civilisation and Christianity. The words of 'Land of Hope and Glory' capture the flavour of these sentiments, though they were not written till the turn of the century;

> Wider still and wider, shall thy bounds be set;
> God who made thee mighty, make thee mightier yet.

Here, then, was a chance for Chamberlain to play a role on the world stage, and this platform was irresistible for such a skilled publicist.

He also believed that there was a strong link between the cause of Empire and social reform. Though his Radical campaigning was behind him, he was still committed to domestic improvement. He believed that removing society's injustices would bind the nation together by lessening class antagonism. One way of finding the money to tackle the evils of chronic poverty and unemployment, was from the profits to be made out of the Empire. He was certain that there were economic opportunities and advantages to be obtained.

HIS ATTITUDE TO EMPIRE

In common with a number of late Victorians he believed that the consolidation and expansion of the Empire offered an escape route from the chronic trade depression which was a feature of the last quarter of the nineteenth century. Foreign competition, falling profits and unemployment were features of Britain's position, and Chamberlain believed that a businesslike restructuring of imperial trade and the proper use of imperial resources offered an unrivalled opportunity for a recovery of British economic vitality. New territories would probably need to be acquired to increase opportunities; certainly, existing ones needed to be fully exploited, as he explained on his acceptance of the Colonial Office in 1895;

> It is because I desire to see whether there may not be room for still

developing our resources in these new countries, and for opening up British markets.

Chamberlain was convinced that Britain benefited from, indeed 'almost lived upon', her Empire. Yet at the high peak of Imperialism, in 1900, trade with the Empire comprised only one-third of our trade with other nations. Such realities did not lessen his enthusiasm, for he could divert discussion into a different realm of argument. Like many other Imperialist spokesmen, he put forward the doctrine of Britain as the 'trustee of civilisation'. It was an ideal of service, a sentiment admirably caught in 'Recessional' in which Kipling; urged his readers to 'take up the White Man's burden', and thereby spread the benefits of the British way of life.

His belief in the missionary duty of the British was linked to his racial beliefs. He believed that the Anglo-Saxons were superior, a 'chosen people' who possessed virtues denied to many other races. Such thinking was again quite typical of the spirit of the times, for there were many who saw their countrymen as a kind of master-race. Robert Louis Stevenson captured something of this mood in his lines;

> Little Indian, Sioux or Crow,
> Little frosty eskimo,
> Little Turk or Japanee
> Oh! don't you wish that you were me?'

For Chamberlain, Britain, with its free, stable, representative institutions, had much to offer 'the lesser breeds without the law'. For the British, Imperial rule was not simply a right, it was something of a moral imperative; the Empire was 'the greatest secular agency for good the world has ever seen'.

His dislike of injustice had long been apparent and he was aware of past mistakes. Too often, he said, previous expansion had been accompanied by unfairness and oppression. He stressed that native property rights should be recognised and that they personally should not be harmed by the coming of white settlers; 'We desire only to enjoy the territories and resources which nations could not use themselves'.

Undertaken in this way and in this spirit, he was sure that the expansion of the Empire was in everybody's interest, and not just a practical means of allowing for the greater prosperity of the British people.

His vision also extended to ideas of an Imperial federation, for such a coming together between the Mother Country and the colonies offered scope for much closer economic and military cooperation. As far back as a speech in Toronto in 1887 he was saying;

> It may yet be that the federation of Canada may be the lamp lighting our path to the federation of the British Empire. If it is a dream – it may be only the imagination of an enthusiast – it is a grand idea. It is an idea to stimulate the patriotism and statesmanship of anyone who loves this country . . . and whether it be destined or not to perfect realisation, at least let us all cherish the sentiment it inspires.

LIFE AT THE COLONIAL OFFICE
—

As the Empire was so scattered and varied, it could never be as responsive to the sort of immediate improvement that Chamberlain was used to securing through his drive and dominating methods. Yet he tackled the task with characteristic energy and resolve, and was to prove an effective minister who could listen to advice, ask the right questions of his officials and make decisions. His gift for gaining publicity was also regularly in evidence, and he was soon confronting MPs with a vast array of documents. But the bustle and noise of a superb propagandist aroused suspicion that the constant movement stemmed more from a campaign of self-promotion than a serious attempt to keep MPs in the picture on the details of important subjects.

At an early stage, he had spoken of developing the undeveloped estates of Empire:

> I regard many of our colonies as being in the condition of undeveloped estates. Cases have already come to my knowledge of colonies which have been British Colonies perhaps for more than a hundred years in which up to the present time British rule has done absolutely nothing. I shall be prepared to consider very carefully myself any case which may occur in which by the judicious investment of British money those estates which belong to the British Crown may be developed for the benefit of their population.

In the coming years, he set about the task enthusiastically. He wished to encourage colonial enterprise on the basis of sound business principles, but here he was in a difficulty. As it was not easy to attract the investment of private capital, he was dependent on the availability of government money, granted in the form of loans. But his policies never received full backing from his Cabinet colleagues, and, more significantly, the Exchequer was reluctant to release an adequate supply of money for his many projects. Greater Prime Ministerial support might have helped in Chamberlain's battle with what Salisbury himself referred to as the 'Gladstonian garrison at the Treasury'.

IMPERIAL REFORM

Imperial reform offered suitable scope for Chamberlain's activity and true to his record, he was interested in the public health in the colonies. He appointed a Medical Adviser to the Colonial Office and, with the assistance of public funds, encouraged the Royal Society to examine tsetse fly infestation; valuable research into this African plague was accomplished.

The study of tropical agriculture and medicine was furthered, and he helped in the establishment of the School of Tropical Medicine in London in 1899, an institution in the forefront of the fight against malaria in Africa. A similar school had opened a little earlier in Liverpool with his support and encouragement, as did an institute for botanical research at Kew which specialised in the study of tropical plants.

He was particularly concerned about the economic weakness of the West Indies, which was overdependent on sugar production. In the late nineteenth century, a prolonged 'bad patch' caused the near ruin of those connected with it, and plantations were left abandoned (including one in which he had invested). Rivalry from the subsidised sugar beet industry of Europe was threatening the livelihood of owners and workers. Chamberlain established a Royal Commission in 1897 to look into economic and social conditions in the region. Its recommendations for a diversification of its production and a more developed economy, with better inter-island communications, were accepted. He even obtained money from the Treasury to fund regular shipping services and improved techniques of agricultural production.

Development loans at low rates of interest were granted to West Africa for the building of railways and harbours, and other 'backward' territories also benefited from the same kind of help. Sometimes action was more dramatic; the Ashanti Kingdom of the Gold Coast was invaded, and after the deposing of the brutal King Prempeh the country was annexed, and human sacrifice and slave trading were abolished.

With such a burst of activity in Africa, it is not surprising that Chamberlain was dubbed 'Joseph Africanus' by contemporary journalists. In addition to such local colonial initiatives, Chamberlain had an ultimate 'grand design'; his goal was imperial integration. Imperial federation had been proposed in the early 1870s, and true believers had even suggested an imperial legislature to which the colonial legislatures and the British Parliament would be subordinate.

At the Colonial Conference held to mark the Diamond Jubilee in 1897, Chamberlain advocated a customs union and a representative Imperial Council, suggestions which were received coolly. All who attended liked the idea of more regular meetings, but any plan which would reduce colonial freedom of action or involve a contribution to imperial defence costs was viewed with scepticism by colonies who had their own plans for self government.

He was also much involved with the six Australian colonies; their need for a common policy over immigration and defence seemed to necessitate some form of federal arrangement. In 1899, a referendum approved the idea and the following year a constitution for a central government was drafted. Chamberlain used his position and influence to persuade the reluctant Western Australia to join, and in 1900 steered the Australian Federation Bill onto the statute book. The passing of the measure was uncontentious, with most MPs agreeing with Chamberlain's observation that:

> whatever is good for Australia is good for the whole British Empire. Therefore, we all of us – independently altogether of party whether at home or in any portion of the Empire – rejoice at this proposal.

He believed that this move was crucial to any plan for imperial federation, though as time elapsed and his experience of office grew, he came to see any such vision was a 'vain and empty dream'. His careful handling of negotiations won him friends among the leaders of the Australian colonies, and as they were on the brink of federation, he was able to urge them to offer voluntary support in Britain's clash with the Boers. 16,000 Australians fought in the Boer War, numerically a modest contribution but a sign that Australia was a willing partner of the Motherland in imperial matters.

However, it was the developments in South Africa that were to dominate his stewardship of the Colonial Office.

THE BACKGROUND TO THE BOER WAR

Much had changed in the Transvaal since the granting of independence in 1881. The discovery of mineral resources, especially gold on the Witwatersrand, had attracted the interests of powerful mining companies, and as rights to construct railways and provide water and other services were granted to overseas investors, vast numbers of skilled workers had moved into the Boer state. The new town of Johannesburg was soon dominated by these foreigners or *Uitlanders*; in the country as a whole, there were probably more adult male non-Boers than Boers.

The Boers, a small pastoral community, were an industrious and sober people, descended from Dutch settlers, much influenced by their Calvinist religious faith. They feared that the character of their state, its language, customs and religion, were under threat from foreign influences. Their President, Paul Kruger, pursued a policy which reflected his low view of the Uitlanders – on the one hand, denying them civil rights whilst, on the other, expecting them to contribute heavily in taxation.

The difficulties experienced by the Uitlanders were not specifically a British problem. Their experiences, however, became part of a larger issue. The British Government was interested in the idea of a union in South Africa. The project was enthusiastically supported by Cecil Rhodes, Prime Minister of Cape Colony after 1890, a millionaire capitalist and imperialist who shared the dream of a vast area of British control in the south of the continent.

Rhodes wanted to bring the Transvaal under British rule and hoped that if it was almost surrounded by British settlers the Boers would be persuaded to join a union. As this plan was unsuccessful, his next hope was to use the grievances of the Uitlanders to overthrow the Boer Government, which might then then be replaced by a new administration more friendly to the mining companies and to Britain. This would put the Transvaal under effective British control.

The failure of his scheme was to involve Joseph Chamberlain in a highly embarrassing situation. The Colonial Secretary's exact role in the events of December 1895 has never been completely unravelled.

The Jameson Raid

In 1895, tension in the Transvaal was building up and the Uitlanders were on the point of rebellion. The mining companies were keen to encourage a rising, and Rhodes and Chamberlain were clearly aware of the likelihood that one would occur. Rhodes was eager to ensure the overthrow of Kruger's Government and sent a force of some 400 volunteer military police under the command of Dr Starr Jameson to Pitsani, in Bechuanaland, adjacent to the Transvaal frontier. From there, to coincide with the uprising, the horsemen could ride to Johannesburg to assist in ensuring its success.

However, things did not go according to plan; there were disputes among the leaders of the Uitlanders. Some were prepared to negotiate with Kruger, having second thoughts about putting themselves under British control. Because of such doubts among the conspirators, the rebellion failed to materialise, and in the circumstances there was no reason for Dr. Jameson and his riders to cross the border in a bid to reach Johannesburg. Yet they did so.

They had insufficient intelligence about the commitment of the Uitlander leaders and the competence of Kruger's force. Forty miles from their goal, the invaders were surrounded by Kruger's commandos and compelled to surrender.

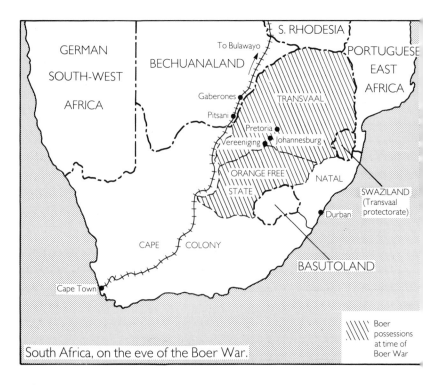

South Africa, on the eve of the Boer War.

The Jameson Raid was a total fiasco, an act of amazing folly. Chamberlain quickly repudiated the Raid, but the Boers became justifiably suspicious of British policy, and the rift between Britain and the Transvaal widened significantly. In other parts of South Africa, the Dutch rallied to Kruger's cause. They may not have liked Kruger, but they certainly now also distrusted Britain and its Colonial Secretary. The President, who received a telegram of congratulations from the German Emperor, Wilhelm II, made preparations for the seemingly inevitable future hostilities.

Chamberlain was in a very embarrassing position. He admitted that he had prior knowledge of the Uitlanders' tentative plans to revolt, but denied knowing of the proposed raid. This is hard to believe, and some evidence undermines Chamberlain's denial. Shortly before the raid the Colonial Office, then under his leadership, agreed to transfer a small portion of the Bechuanaland Protectorate to Rhodes' Company. This was supposed to be used for the building of a railway, but as Jameson's volunteers were shortly stationed in Pitsani, in the town of Gaberones near the Transvaal border, the strong probability is that Chamberlain was aware of Rhodes' objectives and prepared to be involved in his plans.

The likelihood is that Chamberlain was not unhappy that a raid was being prepared, was willing to assist in its planning and believed that there was a possibility that the outcome could be turned to Britain's advantage. When the operation backfired, the Colonial Office stood back and denied any knowledge.

The House of Commons Enquiry

Chamberlain's enemies branded him as an imperial adventurer, while MPs of differing persuasions wanted to know more of the affair. A Select Committee of the House of Commons was set up to investigate the matter, though Chamberlain's presence on it may have intimidated other members.

The Kruger Telegram had made a deep impact on some of them who saw the raiders as heroic figures. As a whole, the Committee proceeded with great caution, nibbling at the evidence and ensuring that nothing emerged which could discredit the Colonial Secretary and, more especially, stain the honour of Britain. In particular, Chamberlain was successful in dissuading the Liberals on the Committee from delving too deeply into several obscure aspects of the affair; skilfully, he exploited their distrust of Rhodes and succeeded in identifying him as the key figure involved.

The enquiry blamed Rhodes as the guilty party and cleared Chamberlain of any involvement. Not surprisingly, some Liberal members felt cheated when in his speech on the Report in July 1897 Chamberlain referred to Rhodes as having made one 'gigantic mistake' in his otherwise entirely noble pursuit of Britain's interests. He passed the blame onto businessmen and government officials much lower down the chain of responsibility.

Many MPs felt that the Committee had been astonishingly gullible and they therefore regarded the enquiry as a sham, a whitewash of the role of the British Government in general, and on Joseph Chamberlain in particular.

Chamberlain, the skilful political operator, much resented the situation in which he found himself. This brought out his fighting instincts, and his dogged defence under pressure may inspire some admiration. However, his behaviour was less than honourable, and the whole affair reflected badly upon him. Some key telegrams which covered the period prior to the Raid and which may well have damaged his defence were never produced in evidence. They could not be obtained, but Chamberlain did not reveal that he had personal copies of many of them. Conscious of the fact that the saga could ruin him, he put pressure on Rhodes' South African Company to uncover as little as possible. The price for their acquiescence was paid in the July speech already mentioned when he vigorously defended Rhodes and described his behaviour as that of a 'man of honour' – having previously signed the Select Committee Report which censured him!

The Approach of War

After this damaging blow to his reputation, Chamberlain still adopted a strong, aggressive approach to Kruger, and had thoughts of revenge. Meanwhile, the Boers were angry with the British Government and deeply suspicious of its intentions. Any chance of a reconciliation of the white races was lost and, in the circumstances, it was almost inevitable that relations between Britain and the Transvaal would deteriorate. The Raid can be seen as a crucial stage in the build-up to war.

Confirmed in their intense dislike of the British, the Boers were keen to find more friends in Southern Africa. They made an alliance with the Orange Free State in 1897, and most Boers in the Cape Colony were also sympathetic to their cause.

Although Britain's position in South Africa was becoming a very uneasy one, Chamberlain's behaviour was not that of a man on the defensive.

Within days of Jameson's surrender, the British High Commissioner, Robinson, was urged to use 'firm language' in pressing again for the rights of the Uitlanders. Robinson believed it was highly unlikely that the exultant Kruger would discuss his state's internal policies. He warned Chamberlain that the President would sooner face war than concede, and that if a military conflict followed then the Dutch in Natal and the Cape Colony would probably rally to his side. In the eyes of the Colonial Secretary, Robinson was too cautious and timid.

A New High Commissioner

In 1897, Chamberlain decided to replace the High Commissioner with someone who shared his belief in Britain's imperial mission, and whose stance might be considerably more belligerent.

The new representative was Sir Alfred Milner, an uncompromising figure who believed that tough measures were needed to restrain Kruger's ascendancy. He was an able administrator, but no diplomat. As British policy stiffened, his presence did nothing to improve the chances of negotiation.

Once Milner had made up his mind, he was stubborn and unmoved. He disliked the Kruger regime intensely, and certainly the President behaved ever more dictatorially after his election victory in 1898. He wrote to Chamberlain that

> there is no way out of the political troubles except reform in the Transvaal or war. And at present, the chances of reform are worse than ever.

He felt that matters were coming to a head and spoke of 'the great day of reckoning' that must surely come.

Chamberlain's own position had been vigorously anti-Boer, but even though he broadly backed Milner, he was worried that events were moving too quickly towards war. Neither the Cabinet nor the public were prepared for this, and no military preparations were in hand.

After the shooting of an English workman by a Boer policeman in December 1898, the Uitlanders were angry when the constable was acquitted. They sent a mammoth petition to Milner. It contained the words; 'The condition of Your Majesty's subjects in this state has become well-nigh intolerable'. At the request of Chamberlain, Milner sent a letter fully explaining his view of the situation now created; it was as strongly worded as the Colonial Secretary had wanted it to be, and contained the following sentence:

> I can see nothing which will put a stop to the mischievous propaganda but some striking proof of the intention of Her Majesty's Government not to be ousted from its position in South Africa.

The Cabinet considered the petition and the letter on May 9, and some ministers were increasingly sympathetic to the Chamberlain-Milner viewpoint. They knew that the Cape was valuable as a naval base, and that British prestige was at stake if the Uitlanders were let down. However, anxieties were expressed about the prospect of war. The Prime Minister believed that the British people and most members of the Government did not favour war 'excepting perhaps Mr Chamberlain'.

Late Negotiations

In late May-early June, negotiations took place at Bloemfontein between Kruger and Milner on the franchise issue. Milner lacked patience with the process of diplomacy, finding the obstinacy and cunning of the Boer President a source of great irritation. Though some concessions were made, he broke off the conference after five days. Chamberlain sent a cable urging Milner to continue talking, but it arrived too late. As a businessman by training, Chamberlain was used to negotiation as a way of solving disputes, even if he did some powerful arm-twisting behind the scenes. He was resourceful in discussion, and could pursue his goals patiently, if resolutely.

Chamberlain still hoped that the Boers might back down, for the High Commissioner led him to believe that the Boers were bluffing. Over the coming months he made several more conciliatory offers and these aroused the interest of moderate Boers in the Transvaal and outside. Such olive-branches foundered on the stubbornness of Kruger who tried to add impossible conditions. He mistrusted Chamberlain even when he was pursuing a more reasonable course. But many in South Africa as well as several members of the House of Commons shared his suspicion.

War Breaks Out

By August, Chamberlain himself was fast losing patience, remarking of Kruger that 'he dribbles out reforms like water from a squeezed sponge'. He made it clear that the 'issues of peace and war' were in the hands of the President, and after the Orange Free State threw in its lot with the Transvaal in late September it seemed inevitable that war would come. It became a question of who first delivered their ultimatum, both sides having a draft prepared. Chamberlain wanted to be able to portray Kruger as the truculent aggressor, and so wished the Boers to take the initiative. The British public would then respond with outrage, and in Britain and the colonies opinion would rally behind the government.

As the Boers seemed better prepared, the timing was in their hands; once the seasonal rains renewed the veldt grass the moment was appropriate for their mounted infantry. On October 9, the day on which the British ultimatum was finalised, the Boers demanded the removal of British troops from the border of the Transvaal and a halt to reinforcements. The Colonial Secretary rejected this, and the Transvaal began the Boer War with pre-emptive military strikes.

For Chamberlain, what was at stake was:

> the position of Great Britain in South Africa, and with it the estimate formed of our power and influence in our colonies and throughout the world.

He was not unhappy at the outcome, whereas Lord Salisbury could not disguise his anxiety. Relations between them had been uneasy for many months, with frequent disagreements over foreign and colonial policies, and differences in their general approach to affairs. Chamberlain liked to portray himself as the Cabinet's strong man; he was aware of patriotic feeling on the back benches and in the jingoistic popular press, and never much cared for the cautious and sceptical attitude of the Prime Minister.

Chamberlain's handling of events had been uncertain. He had pursued no consistent line, sometimes sounding menacing to the Transvaal, at other times conciliatory; sometimes, he had spoken with threats and ultimatums, at others he seemed genuinely to want an agreement. He miscalculated the Boer state of mind, for he anticipated a climb-down by Kruger, believing that the President would not be prepared to go to war. Yet because Chamberlain had not been calling for military preparations it was easy for Kruger to remain obstinate, doubtful if Britain was resolved to fight for the rights of the Uitlanders.

Nonetheless, because he had not been consistently bellicose, it was easier for Unionists, Liberal Imperialists and the centre of the Liberal party to offer backing to his position when war finally came. From the colonies, the only voices critical of Chamberlain were those of spokesmen who thought he could have been tougher with the Transvaal. This enabled him to make the doubtful claim in the House of Commons that 'from the first day I came into office, I hoped for peace; I strove for peace'. His performance was very effective, for despite the inner doubts among some of those present, few, even of his political opponents, spoke against him.

The Radicals, often criticised as 'pro-Boer', had no doubts that it was 'Chamberlain's War'. Lloyd George, previously an admirer of Chamberlain in spite of their disagreements, boldly dared to attack both Chamberlain and the Government. Others echoed a Gladstonian spirit, seeing the war as fundamentally ill-conceived. Morley's forecast of what might result contained more than a grain of truth: 'It will bring you no glory. It will bring you no profit, but mischief, and it will be wrong'.

THE WAR, 1899-1902

Between them, Chamberlain and Milner had created a situation in which, despite the reluctance of Salisbury and other colleagues, war was difficult to avoid if a major humiliation was to be averted. Chamberlain was aware of the unease which many people had felt. In December 1899, he told Milner that:

> It was all very well for you and me to know, as we did, what a tremendous issue was behind such questions as franchise and alien immigration; but the public did not. They could not see that the things we were contending for were worth a big war, nor were they particularly pleased with the clients on whose behalf we appeared to be acting. There was too much 'money bags' about the whole business to be agreeable to any of us.

Britain's military inadequacy was quickly exposed, and forced Chamberlain to issue a series of urgent directives. By contrast, the skilful Boer horsemen, fighting on the home territory of the veldt, soon displayed their superior technique and scored several convincing victories*. Such British setbacks actually helped Chamberlain's case, for pledges of assistance came from across the Empire and Australia, New Zealand and Canada rallied to

---

* For further details on the course of events, see pages 30-1 in Chapter 2.

the call. Chamberlain saw their willing contribution to the war effort as a vindication of his diplomacy, and an endorsement of his emphasis on Imperial unity.

Though the opposition tried to exploit the government's position, blaming Chamberlain personally for the war, the Liberals were so seriously divided in their tactics and approach that the Colonial Secretary could ride out any disagreement. After the humiliations of 1899, the tide turned, and by the summer of 1900 things looked better from the military point of view. The rest of the war was mainly a series of guerilla actions.

The Government called an election, enabling it to cash in on its recent victories. The Liberals, divided over the war, lost a few seats in this 'Khaki Election' in which Chamberlain was bound to be a major performer. He set out to vindicate his role, past and present, and to build up popular support. No-one on the Tory side could match his contribution, either in quality or quantity, as with great vigour he defended his reputation. He fought hard, as always, and Beatrice Webb commented that he 'played down low to the 'man in the street''.

The one Liberal who could effectively counter-attack was Lloyd George. In the campaign, he presumed to denounce Chamberlain's backers whose business interests had flourished in the war. His sharp observation that 'the more the Empire expands, the more the Chamberlains contract' was a telling one. He was denounced as 'pro-Boer', whereas other Liberals were keen to portray themselves as 'anti-Joe, but never pro-Kruger'. Not surprisingly, when the Welshman boldly tried to address an anti-war gathering in Chamberlain's Birmingham base, in 1901, he was lucky to escape with his life. Angry Chamberlain supporters mobbed the building, and in the chaos, Lloyd George was only able to escape when disguised as a policeman!

The next two years were difficult, for ending the war proved to be a prolonged business. British tactics, including the burning of farms, the use of concentration camps and the delay in securing ultimate victory, all helped to discredit the notion of Empire. The optimism of late-Victorian imperialism had received a sharp setback, and as the new century dawned, the more blatant expressions of Imperial sentiment common at the beginning of the war were to be a thing of the past.

The war was costly in money and life, but when the fighting was over the terms of the settlement at Vereeniging in May 1902 were generous. The Orange Free State and the Transvaal were absorbed into the British

Empire, but the Afrikaans language was allowed in schools and the courts. Hope was held out to the Boers for future self-government, and a relief grant was made available for reconstruction. The generosity of the outcome made improved relations more likely, and Joseph Chamberlain's phraseology reflected the desire to work together harmoniously as he spoke of reconciliation; 'We are one nation under one flag . . . We have left the past behind'.

timeline	1895	Appointed as Colonial Secretary
	1897	Colonial Conference; supported closer Imperial union
	1900	Australian Federation Act

In South Africa

1895 Dec	Jameson Raid
1897 May	Report of Select Committee issued
Aug	Milner appointed as High Commisioner
1899 March	Uitlander petition presented
May	Bloemfontein Conference
Oct	Boer War began
1902 May	Peace of Vereeniging

Points to consider

1) **Why was Chamberlain so interested in the Colonial Secretaryship? What were his beliefs about the value of the British Empire?**
2) **Excluding events in South Africa, in which areas if Imperial policy did he gain success and in which did he fail?**
3) **How much criticism does his behaviour over the Jameson Raid merit, and what light, if any, does it throw on his character?**
4) **Consider the events leading up to the Boer War in the light of Salisbury's belief that he was a warmonger?**
5) **He later said that the war was, at some point, inevitable. Do you agree?**
6) **In what senses can the Boer War justly be described as 'Chamberlain's War'?**
7) **What benefits, if any, did the Empire bring to Great Britain in the late nineteenth century?**

8

TARIFF REFORM AND
A UNIONIST DEFEAT

For several years, Chamberlain had felt that Free Trade was a hindrance to economic recovery. If Britain was to regain its former industrial vigour, and increase national prosperity and strength, he believed this had to be done in the context of its relationship to the Empire. 'The creation of an Empire such as the world has ever seen . . .' was his dream, and a new approach on the question of tariffs could help to cement the union of Britain and the colonial governments.

In the last Budget of the Salisbury Ministry, the Chancellor had reimposed a registration duty on corn, grain, meal and flour as one of several measures to finance the rising costs of war. This one shilling duty was soon denounced by the Liberals for it opened the door to some return of protectionism. Its unpopularity, however, did not deflect Chamberlain from further discussion of British trading policy.

Indeed, as his local party was at that time unhappy about the religious clauses of the government's Education Bill, there was much to be said for diverting attention to the subject of the business prosperity of Birmingham and the nation as a whole. In a speech which referred to Britain's isolation, he warned that

> The intention is to shut out this country . . . from all profitable trade . . . and . . . to enable those foreign states to undersell us in British markets . . . the days are for great Empires, not for little states.

Chamberlain chaired the Colonial Conference of June-August 1902, though his role was mainly a listening one. He did put forward his idea of an Imperial Council, but the assembled statesmen were unenthusiastic about any plan which placed increased financial and military burdens upon their states. They were more receptive to his remarks on Imperial Preference, especially the Canadian Prime Minister, who showed much interest when Chamberlain took up this theme.

New Zealand, Australia and Canada wished to protect and improve the living standards of their own people and develop their own industries. Tariffs on imports were the obvious means of safeguarding their position. They might be willing to lower such duties on goods coming in from Britain if the Mother Country could offer some preferential treatment to their exports, notably of food and raw materials. Such a scheme was dependent on Britain having some existing duties to relax, so that the colonies could benefit from a reciprocal deal.

The corn duty gave Chamberlain the opportunity to explore these possibilities. To abandon this tariff on colonial goods whilst retaining it on corn from outside the Empire meant a breach with British policy which had been accepted by all parties for over a half a century. Yet such a change in fiscal policy offered a real possibility of closer commercial union within the Empire, and a move towards that more general imperial integration of which he dreamed.

He took the issue to Cabinet in the autumn of 1902, hoping that the new Chancellor, Ritchie, might be on his side. The outcome was uncertain as Ritchie wanted more time for the Treasury to consider the proposal; he was reluctant to abandon Free Trade. Though the Cabinet was generally sympathetic to some policy of preferential tariffs, Ritchie reserved the right to have the issue reopened nearer to the time of his next Budget.

After Chamberlain set off for South Africa to bring about reconciliation after the end of the Boer War, Ritchie acted on the tariff question and outmanoeuvred him. He decided to abandon the Corn Tax altogether, and thus removed the possibility of Britain offering preference to colonial exporters. This was a devastating blow to Chamberlain, for the Cabinet accepted the proposal, knowing that the Chancellor had threatened to resign should it be rejected. In particular, Balfour was reluctant to lose Ritchie so close to the Budget.

On his return from Africa, Chamberlain seemed tired and unwell, and he failed to pursue the question. If the Prime Minister had been forced to choose between Ritchie and his Colonial Secretary, he must surely have opted for Chamberlain who was the most important member of the Cabinet. If Ritchie had gone, Chamberlain could almost certainly have edged his colleagues round to a more protectionist stance. Yet he seemed too weary to fight, the more so as he had not even begun to popularise his ideas on Imperial Preference. He felt he could return to the subject on another occasion. Meanwhile some Ministers were not sorry to see him successfully taken on by a lesser public figure, much his junior.

A NEW CAUSE – TARIFF REFORM

For several months, Chamberlain had been in low spirits. He was depressed about the political situation, for the government was showing signs of exhaustion after eight years in office; the Liberals, after their difficulties in the war, were beginning to poll more strongly. He had been a target of persistent criticism, and felt a sense of frustration at not being able to achieve as much as he wanted. He needed a new cause, and Tariff Reform fitted the bill admirably.

A bold initiative was called for, and on 15 May he made one of his most famous and significant speeches. He invoked the Imperial spirit in his call for fiscal reform, for he observed; 'The Empire is in its infancy. Now is the time when we can mould that Empire'. He argued that Free Trade had been appropriate in the past, but by now world conditions had changed in a way 'never contemplated by any of those whom we regard as the authors of Free Trade'. In this new situation, the old orthodoxies were irrelevant and a policy of Imperial Preference would consolidate the Empire 'by relations of interest as well as relations of sentiment'.

The effect of such remarks was dramatic. No longer could the issue be tackled gradually, step by step. Instead, a head-on assault on Free Trade was to be launched. Though some young Unionists were enthusiastic, inspired by such an Imperial vision, others were unhappy, especially some of the Liberal Unionists previously committed to that doctrine.

The Prime Minister, Balfour, was in an appalling dilemma. Faced by disunity on the backbenches and in the Cabinet, he strove desperately to hold the party together. A contemporary jingle pointed to his indecision:

> I'm not for Free Trade, and I'm not for Protection.
> I approve of them both, and to both have objection.

Actually, his own inclinations veered towards a form of protectionism. He had been doubtful about the wisdom of Free Trade for some time, and saw that the issue was ripe for reconsideration. Retaliatory tariffs against countries who blocked British exports and Imperial Preference to bind the Empire together were desirable as long as he had time to win over the waverers; 'The thing is worth getting if you can get it without paying too heavily'.

He asked his Cabinet colleagues not to go public on the matter, hoping that it could be left until after the next election. Meanwhile, Chamberlain was spreading information via his Birmingham machine. He set up a Tariff Reform Committee locally, as well as a nationwide Tariff Reform League with the backing of several academics, businessmen and journalists.

Though he was gaining supporters in the country, his cause was making less progress in the Cabinet. Balfour was at times irritated by the way Chamberlain used every opportunity to exploit the issue and give it a high profile. He did not directly challenge the Government, but found it increasingly difficult to go along with the truce. Indeed, the Cabinet was speaking with many different voices, and by September there was a crisis which had to be resolved as both sides found the situation intolerable.

Balfour could hesitate no longer. His leadership was under attack from both wings of the Conservative Party, and he was portrayed by many critics as a fence-sitter, incapable of making up his mind or giving a clear lead. His attempt to steer a middle course had ultimately pleased no-one, for the wound was too open to be healed by reassuring words.

RESIGNATION
—

The outcome of the Cabinet crisis was that Chamberlain resigned, as did three convinced Free Traders. After the inevitable Cabinet reshuffle, there were few committed Chamberlain supporters at the higher level. However, the situation was certainly an odd one, for Austen Chamberlain replaced Ritchie at the Exchequer. As Campbell-Bannerman remarked:

> This plan of Joe outside, and Arthur working inside with 'our Mr Austen' in charge of the counting-house is too bare-faced for anything.

Chamberlain's resignation was on the surface an agreed strategy, both players accepting the other's position, and the need to act accordingly. Whatever Balfour's personal leanings, above all, he wished to keep the Conservatives and their Liberal Unionist allies in power for as long as possible. The alternative was the return of the Liberals who might well take up Home Rule again; if dependent on Labour backing, they might open the way to the advance of socialism. Neither could be contemplated.

Austen Chamberlain later suggested that Balfour had 'encouraged' his father to leave the government. In a sense, this was true; the resignation suited him in the difficult circumstances in which he found himself. He was in broad agreement with Chamberlain, but needed time to win the Cabinet doubters round. Chamberlain could accept this, for he admitted that his ideas were 'politically impracticable' for the time being. Indeed, when the King assumed that there were political differences between the two men and that these were the cause of the resignation, Chamberlain responded that 'Mr Balfour and his present colleagues agree with Mr Chamberlain'.

From Chamberlain's point of view, the advantages of departure were questionable. He could have stayed in the Cabinet and fought alongside his son and other supporters. The threat of a mass defection might well have produced a major concession; if not, there may have been such a split that the Government would have fallen. If a resulting election was lost, Chamberlain could then hope to reorganise the party and convert it to his programme. It is hard to believe that personal friendship with the Prime Minister would have prevented him from threatening the Government in this way. This was not the Chamberlain style, for once convinced of his position he always campaigned aggressively for it.

What Chamberlain wanted was the opportunity to launch a countrywide appeal to the voters, to capture them for his cause. He believed that he could obtain popular backing as he had so often done in his earlier and more Radical days. Freedom from departmental responsibilities would give him the opportunity to plan his campaign. Furthermore, it would give him a break from the cares of office, the strain of which he was finding irksome. Resignation and an appeal to the electorate would provide a spur for a person much attracted to the idea of a new crusade.

CHAMBERLAIN'S PROGRAMME

In his new role as the apostle of Tariff Reform, Chamberlain plunged into a heavy programme of commitments. He made a series of major speeches in the towns and cities up and down the country in what was a new type of political campaign. When Gladstone had toured the country to crusade against the injustices of Turkish rule in Bulgaria, he was denouncing what

a note on . . .

BRITAIN'S TRADING POSITION

Mid-Nineteenth Century

Britain adopted Free Trade, which
- enabled food to be imported freely, to feed a growing population.
- enabled raw materials to be imported freely; these could then be turned into manufactured goods, and re-exported around the world.

The policy was widely supported and thought to be basic to Britain's commercial success and economic prosperity.

Late Nineteenth Century

Some doubts were being expressed from the 1880s onwards. By 1900, several countries, such as Germany, the United States, France, Italy and Russia, were adopting protective tariffs. These enabled home industries to develop and flourish behind the tariff wall.

As Germany and other countries became efficient producers of manufactured goods, their salesmen could sell in British markets. Often they could undercut the prices charged by British firms, and this foreign competition was a threat to several industries; e.g., German buttons and screws could often be found in the Midlands, where similar British items were traditionally made.

Chamberlain's Answer

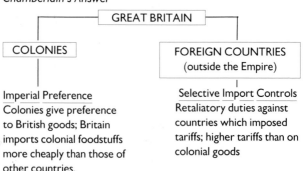

| GREAT BRITAIN |

| COLONIES | | FOREIGN COUNTRIES (outside the Empire) |

Imperial Preference
Colonies give preference to British goods; Britain imports colonial foodstuffs more cheaply than those of other countries.

Selective Import Controls
Retaliatory duties against countries which imposed tariffs; higher tariffs than on colonial goods

BUT Much of Britain's food supply came from outside the Empire, especially grain. Chamberlain's policy meant higher bread prices; FREE TRADE = CHEAP BREAD.

was known to be happening at the time. In Chamberlain's case, he was offering the key to prosperity in the future, showing what life could be like if his programme was implemented. These benefits were speculative and had to be balanced against the risks involved in abandoning Free Trade.

The proposals for Imperial Preference had already been outlined in his Birmingham speech. In his campaign propaganda, he stressed that he wished to see lower tariffs on imported foodstuffs from within the Empire in order to benefit the colonies. In addition, he wanted to see retaliatory duties against foreign competitors to persuade them to remove their barriers to British exports:

> These tariffs, designed to exclude British manufactures, have enabled foreign producers to undersell the British manufacturer in neutral markets and even to attack his home trade . . . The Tariff Reformers believe that by rearming ourselves with the weapon of a moderate tariff, we may still defend our home market against unfair competition, and may secure a modification of foreign tariffs which would open the way to a fairer exchange of products than we have hitherto been able to obtain.

The policy was not a total rejection of Free Trade in favour of full-blooded protection. Rather, it involved a selective use of import controls combined with a lowering of hurdles for countries within the Empire. Of course, his critics were able to portray his ideas as a dangerous departure, and they soon pointed out that tariffs on imported corn would mean dearer bread.

He urged that Tariff Reform would not only be of benefit to British industry but would actually help working people. He well understood the importance of converting them to his side, remarking in May 1905:

> Unless I have the support of the working people, clearly my movement is already condemned and utterly a failure.

The three main planks of his appeal to working men were:

- Firstly, that the Empire was beneficial to the working class. It offered a market for British goods, creating openings for workers at home, in addition to the added prospect of employment being available in the colonies. The *Daily Express* blazoned the caption: 'Tariff Reform Means Work For All'.
- Secondly, he attempted to arouse popular support by appealing to their love of country; 'England without an Empire would not be the England we love'.

Chamberlain addressing a meeting at Bingley Hall; he is demonstrating that there was little difference in size between Protectionist and Free Trade loaves.

• Thirdly, claiming that the causes of Empire and social reform were related, he suggested that Tariff Reform would lead to improvement in domestic living and working conditions. The theory was that on the profits manufacturers made in the Empire, tax would be paid which could finance reforming measures such as Old Age Pensions.

While Chamberlain tended to emphasise the employment benefits, his working-class audiences still associated Free Trade with a lower cost of living. His opponents had made skilful propaganda use of the contrast between the 'big loaf' they could afford now, and the 'little loaf' they would be eating in the future. Cheap bread had a more immediate appeal than any potential prospects for jobs. The second argument could no longer be taken for granted in the aftermath of the Boer War, for patriotic feeling among all classes lacked some of its earlier strength. The third point was less stressed, and it was difficult for Chamberlain to put flesh on the bones of his vague proposals. His Liberal opponents could offer far more in the way of social legislation, and nothing in the last few years suggested that it was only money which prevented the Unionists from taking up the social theme.

THE CAMPAIGN

Chamberlain's personal contribution to the campaign was tireless, as he addressed his very diverse audiences with boundless enthusiasm. Often his own approach in vast public meetings was demagogic, whereas others in the Tariff Reform Committee presented their carefully researched findings in a very different way. Between them, they saturated the Edwardian public with information, via doorstep visits, a mass of leaflets and popular music-hall ditties. Chamberlain was familiar with recent American campaigning techniques, some of which he employed. In particular, Chamberlain's own voice was recorded on gramophone to be played at the gatherings he could not address himself, in public houses and at local meetings.

Yet with all this activity, the results were disappointing. He was not as successful as he hoped in convincing the electorate, for the more the campaign developed the more alarmed many electors became. They were anxious at the 'stomach tax' being proposed, and found it hard to believe in future benefits which might anyway prove illusory. Opinion was also overwhelmingly against him in Whitehall, particularly in the Treasury. Free Trade had been the accepted wisdom for many years, and the doubts of officials about abandoning it were echoed by most leading economists.

A poster issued by the Imperial Tariff Committee Birmingham. Tariff reform and fear of the foreigner.

With many other groups and individuals having such doubts, the impact on the Conservative Party was very serious. Its own dissensions were evident among MPs and within the party organisation. Many accepted Balfour's view that Imperial Preference was impracticable at that time, and there was no sign that the 1903-4 winter campaign had weakened the leader's own belief that it was his primary task to keep the party together. Poor by-election results in 1904 showed the price of disunity, though tariffs were by no means the only issue on which the government was losing popularity. The Tariff Reformers themselves recognised that they were not making the headway anticipated, and morale was in decline by the end of the year.

A major factor in the declining fortunes of the Conservatives and their allies was the revitalisation of their Liberal opponents. Whereas in the past, it was the Liberals who had appeared to be divided and vacillating, they were now hammered into a new unity by Chamberlain's activities. Liberal leader Herbert Asquith followed Chamberlain around the country, and addressed meetings in which he countered his arguments point by point. Many contemporaries noted that Chamberlain lost the intellectual battle to his pursuer.

The relationship between Balfour and Chamberlain began to deteriorate. Chamberlain believed that, in the next election, the Unionists would be defeated. He wanted that event to come as soon as possible, with the issue being his tariff programme. Assuming that the Liberals would form the new government and that their administration would soon run into difficulties, he felt that the public would then be ready to accept his proposals. Such a strategy had little appeal to Balfour who was not keen to hold an election which would result in his loss of office.

Chamberlain and his son Austen both pressed Balfour for more of a movement towards their position, urging him on with reminders that elections 'are won by enthusiasm, they are lost by timidity'. They pointed out that of the Unionist MPs, the majority were strongly in favour of preferential and/or retaliatory tariffs, that most of the others could be sympathetic if the Government came out in favour and that there were only 27 committed Free Traders, some of whom were on the point of retirement.

Balfour's appeals for unity were ignored, as Chamberlain wanted the Prime Minister to speak out decisively. He felt that Balfour's tactics were humiliating, and that there was little to be gained from being a supporter of a government which behaved with such impotence. Chamberlain continued to urge his leader to adopt a more vigorous approach and give a protectionist lead. Recognising the widespread dissatisfaction in his party and the difficulty of steering it through another Parliamentary session, Balfour decided that it was time to resign office; in December, the Liberals took over and called for new elections.

THE 1906 ELECTION

Polling took place in January 1906 and aroused much interest; there was a high (80 per cent) turnout, and a close contest in almost every constituency.

When the first results were announced, it was obvious that there was going to be a landslide Liberal victory. At an early stage, Balfour was defeated and several other Cabinet members also lost their seats. In every area of the country the Unionists were routed, with the single exception of the West Midlands where they actually polled more votes than their opponents.

Some Chamberlainites, such as the future leader and Prime Minister, Bonar Law, were defeated, but Chamberlain could take comfort from the good results in Birmingham where the seven seats were held – in most cases, with an increased majority. The Birmingham Unionists were all Tariff Reformers, and he (and his son Austen in East Worcestershire) fared particularly well. The oft-employed skill of Joseph Chamberlain in organising successful election campaigns had again delivered the goods. This aspect was noted in the contemporary press which blamed some of the party's poor showing on a run-down in party organisation after a decade of office.

The overall result was disastrous for the Unionists as a whole. Whereas their opponents won 377 seats, they retained only 157. Chamberlain could take heart from the fact that, of these, 109 were on his side and 32 were Balfourians who might move in the direction of protection. However, the loss of support in almost all areas and among all classes in the community, indicated a massive rejection of Unionist policies. Deficient party organisation may have increased the number of losses but hardly accounts for such a comprehensive defeat.

To Free Traders and Balfourians in the party, the explanation was obvious; Chamberlain's insistence in pursuing the tariff question had caused dissension in the party. In the process, he had upset working-class voters who feared dearer food, and middle-class ones who were anxious about the repercussions of such a major change in accepted fiscal policy. In particular, an important by-product of this single-minded obsession was the way in which it had helped to reunite the Liberal Party, which benefited from a national swing of around 9 per cent. Many who in the Khaki Election of 1900 had felt disinclined to turn out and vote for the divided Liberals, now felt inspired to do so. As the defenders of Free Trade, they had a popular and successful rallying cry; this was especially true in such areas as Lancashire where trade was highly significant to local prosperity.

Some Conservative and Unionist Free Traders felt particularly venomous about Chamberlain and his role in the defeat. Apart from their differences over tariffs, members of the aristocratic Cecil family revealed something of their distaste for Chamberlain, his background and style. To Lord Robert Cecil, his whole approach to politics was anathema; 'It appears to be utterly sordid and materialistic, not yet corrupt but on the high road to corruption'.

The party was suffering from a fatigue to which governments long in office are prone, and for Chamberlain this exhaustion was the main explanation. There was a shortage of ideas, and a general sense of drift. Balfour must take some of the blame for this; whatever his gifts as a parliamentarian, he was 'a dexterous, rather than a compelling leader'. He seemed remote from the mass of people, as Austen Chamberlain noted; 'He has no comprehension of the thoughts and habits of his countrymen, and no idea of how things strike them'. He had no programme to rouse popular interest or enthusiasm; indeed, it was partly because of the lack of a sense of direction that Chamberlain had felt impelled to take up his new cause.

Chamberlain's own verdict on the election result was clear:

> Personally, I should place the reasons for defeat in the following order;
> 1 General weariness of a Government which had practically been in power for twenty years, and had become stale, and the consequent apathy among its supporters.
> 2 Objection, especially among the Dissenters, to the Education policy of the Government.
> 3 The intense feelings aroused against the employment of Chinese labour.
> 4 The fears of the Trade Unionists that their funds are endangered by a recent decision of the Court of Appeal'.

Some of the decisions taken by the government had been certainly unpopular, particularly those over the Education Act and Chinese slavery. It was, of course, convenient for Tariff Reformers to blame such things for the defeat, for it diverted attention from the electoral albatross of their own campaign. Actually, the swing to the Liberals was not notably greater in Nonconformist areas than elsewhere, though it is true that the Act so deeply offended that group that the issue was another factor which helped to put the Liberal Party back into fighting shape.

Chamberlain had been unhappy about rate-aid for Church schools from the start, and when convinced by Morant that financial assistance was necessary he had suggested direct state-aid instead. He believed that this measure was an electoral liability, but, of course, as he remained in the Cabinet he must bear his share of collective responsibility.

He also had serious misgivings about the question of Chinese slavery. In South Africa, he had made known his opposition to Milner's proposal to import indentured Chinese coolies because of the shortage of labour in the mines of the Rand; he noted that 'such action . . . would raise a storm at home'. As Colonial Secretary, he had rejected the scheme, but after his resignation his successor had given the British Government's consent. This new policy was to be much exploited by Liberal and Labour politicians in 1905-6, on both humanitarian and economic grounds. However, Chamberlain must be cleared of any responsibility for this particular affront to the feelings of many members of the working and middle-classes.

Moreover, if he had had his way, the election would have come sooner. In mid-1905, he told Balfour that he 'should have dissolved two years ago', to which his Leader replied; 'Well, I suppose you are right'. Certainly, this may well have reduced the size of the Liberal victory, for the full extent of Unionist dissension would not have yet become apparent. Of course, Chamberlain did not fear such an election as he was reconciled to the idea of his party's inevitable defeat.

Increasingly, however, the view of modern historians has been to see the 'labour question' as the vital issue in the election. On social reform, the Balfour Government could offer little, and, indeed, since 1895 nothing had been done to win the working-classes over to the Unionist cause. Yet by now they were becoming a decisive element in the fortunes of political parties, an importance which had in the past been concealed by such issues as Home Rule or 'Chamberlain's War'. In 1906, without those distracting issues, these voters could make their desires known, and they did so by voting

Liberal, 'Lib-Lab' (Liberal and Labour party alliance) or for the Independent Labour candidates. Certainly, the Unionist working-class vote was sharply down. The 'Lib-Lab' agreement that Labour and Liberal candidates would not oppose each other perhaps made the result more decisive. It meant that electors could opt for the anti-Unionist candidate with the greater chance of success.

If there was one issue which had really upset the working classes, especially those in the trade unions, it was the Taff Vale case. The judgement of the House of Lords in 1901 had established the principle that a union could be sued by a company for any losses it had incurred as a result of a strike. Trade unions had felt that they were free of such liability, and this interpretation of the law put their funds in jeopardy; it could ruin any union that took industrial action.

They looked to Parliament for legislation to restore their freedom of action, but the Balfour Ministry offered nothing immediate to deal with the impact of this damaging judicial decision. It only set up a Royal Commission, whereas other parties by contrast were pledged to remove the grievance. On this matter, Chamberlain, the ex-Radical, was blind to the need to remove the threat to the union's legal position. Nor had he been as active as was necessary in seeking to convince trade union representatives of the advantages for them of fiscal reform.

THE AFTERMATH OF DEFEAT

Whatever the cause of the catastrophe of 1906, Chamberlain was personally in a strong position early that year. Apart from the satisfaction of winning his own seat handsomely (while Balfour and other ex-Ministers had suffered rebuffs) he could see his supporters well represented on the Conservative and Unionist side of the House. His standing was inevitably great, and if he had wished to grasp the leadership whilst Balfour was out of Parliament, the opportunity was there.

He made no such attempt, believing that restoring the party's fortunes without Balfour's influence would be a daunting task. Instead, he was unusually conciliatory, knowing that Balfour was in no position to dictate the terms of future policy. On February 14, 1906, the two men published the 'Valentine's Day Accord', a truce the party much needed. Though fiscal reform was unlikely for the foreseeable future, the ex-Prime Minister acknowledged its importance as 'the first constructive work of the Unionist

Party'. This safeguarded his leadership, and Chamberlain urged his supporters to campaign on Balfour's behalf at an early by-election.

At the very time when Chamberlain could almost certainly have taken the leadership without much struggle, he had revealed a marked reluctance to steal a march on his old colleagues. By then, his ambitions had been as fulfilled as they were likely to be. At the age of 70, a bitter and possibly inconclusive fight against elements within his own party held little attraction for him.

timeline	1902 June-Aug	Colonial Conference
	1903 May	Major speech on Tariff Reform
	Sept	Resignation from Balfour Government
	1905 Dec	Resignation of Balfour Government
	1906 Jan	General Election; landslide Liberal win
	Feb	Valentine's Day Accord

Points to consider

1) What form of revised trading arrangements did Chamberlain favour?
2) Why do you think that he was unable to convince his Cabinet colleagues of the need for such changes?
3) He resigned from the Cabinet in September 1903 over tariff reform. What benefits were there in resignation, and what disadvantages?
4) What benefits did he see for working people in his policy of tariff reform, and why were they so sceptical about its advantages?
5) Consider the effectiveness of Balfour's handling of the tariff question, between 1902 and 1905. How would you defend him against the charge made in the contemporary rhyme below?

   'I'm not for Free Trade, and I'm not for Protection
   I approve of them both, and to both have objection.
   In going through life I continually find
   It's a terrible business to make up one's mind.
   So in spite of all comments, reproach and convictions,
   I firmly adhere to Unsettled Convictions.'
6) Do you think that Balfour treated Chamberlain fairly over the issue?
7) Consider Chamberlain's version of the causes for the Unionist defeat in 1906. Are they an eloquent explanation? Can he be exonerated from the bulk of any explanation? Can he be exonerated from the bulk of any blame for the defeat?
8) Do you think that Free Trade had ceased to be appropriate in late nineteenth century Britain?

9

LAST YEARS

After the 1906 election, Chamberlain acted as Leader of the Opposition until Balfour returned to the House. He still enjoyed political life, on the hustings and at Westminster, but the strain was beginning to tell. He told his son Neville early in the year:

> I cannot go at half speed. I must either do my utmost or stop altogether and though I know of the risks I prefer to take them.

He had been troubled by blinding headaches for some time and Neville felt that he was near to collapse. In March, after delivering a major speech in his home town, he had a minor stroke which temporarily left him unable to speak. He recovered and was soon much cheered by the news that other son Austen had become engaged to be married.

In early July, he celebrated his seventieth birthday and also thirty years as an MP for Birmingham. The city was keen to mark the events and a luncheon at the Council House was followed by a procession and firework display in his honour. At Bingley Hall, 10,000 enthusiastic supporters gathered to hear him speak, and the warmth of their affection was apparent to all observers.

He was on good form as he made a speech which looked back over his long career. He spoke passionately and confidently, and in his conclusion urged that:

> The union of the Empire must be preceded and accompanied by a better understanding, by a closer sympathy. To secure that is the highest object of statesmanship now at the beginning of the twentieth century; and, if these were the last words that I were permitted to utter unto you, I would rejoice to utter them in your presence and with your approval. I know that the fruition of our hopes is certain. I hope I may live to congratulate you upon our

common triumph; but, in any case, I have a faith in the people. I trust in the good sense, in the intelligence and the patriotism of the majority, the vast majority, of my countrymen. I look forward to the future with hope and confidence, and

'others I doubt not, if not we
the issue of our toil shall see'.

His choice of words was to prove remarkably prophetic for, back in London to attend a meeting of the Tariff Commission, he told a friend 'I am a wreck'. That evening, dressing for dinner, he suffered a massive stroke which completely paralysed the right side of his body, depriving him of movement and speech.

There was some improvement in his sight and speech when he returned to Highbury. For a while, he even felt that he might overcome his infirmity, but within a few years it was obvious to everyone that he would never recover. For one so active and determined, this was a devastating realisation.

His mind remained alert and, in spite of his incapacity, he liked to receive visits from former colleagues and retained a lively interest in current politics. His constituents in West Birmingham remained loyal and he was elected unopposed in the two elections of 1910. When the House reassembled at the beginning of the new year, he was carried into the Chamber once the rest of the MPs had departed. There, he was formally sworn in, a scene vividly described by one eye-witness:

For a few moments he sat, piteously but proudly motionless, whilst his eye surveyed the empty benches and galleries, and then he indistinctly repeated the Oath after the Clerk. To sign the Roll was for him a physical impossibility, but Austen guided his hand sufficiently to make a shaky cross, and then, after another poignant pause, we carried him out again. As he passed the Chair, the Speaker leaned over to touch his helpless hand, and the tragic ceremony was over.

He lingered on, a rather pathetic figure, lovingly looked after by his wife and daughters. He wintered in Cannes, and was wheeled up and down the promenade. At home, he was utterly dependent in his final months; as Neville remarked, 'He who had been so self-reliant was now dependent on a woman for every common act of life'. He took pleasure in his grandchildren and tried to attract and amuse them, but his slurred words and grunts tended to frighten those who could not understand.

In January 1914, he announced that he would not stand for Parliament again, and Austen replaced him as candidate for West Birmingham. A farewell garden party was held at Highbury in May, and soon afterwards he went to London at his own request. He believed that his advice might be needed in the coming months for the third Home Rule Bill would shortly reach the statute book. He offered this view to Sir Edward Carson and Lord Halsbury, when they visited him; 'don't give in . . . fight it out to the end'.

On July 2, he suffered a major heart attack and died in his wife's arms. His family rejected the offer of burial in Westminster Abbey, and instead he was laid to rest at Key Hill cemetery Birmingham following a service in the Church of the Messiah. The streets of Birmingham were crowded, shops displayed black-edged photographs in the windows and flags were flown at half-mast. For personal and political associates and friends, a memorial service was held at St. Margaret's, Westminster.

His widow did not return to Birmingham. She was present with Austen, Hilda and Ida at the centenary celebrations organised in the Albert Hall in 1936. Neville addressed the local commemoration in the Town Hall, and many residents in the second city could endorse his tribute to 'Brummagem Joe':

> The greatest service of Joseph Chamberlain to local government was the setting of it on a new pedestal of dignity and honour. Joseph Chamberlain always held municipal work as one of the most honourable and useful a vocation that any man or woman could follow. In honouring him today, Birmingham is honouring herself and falsifying the saying that a prophet is not without honour except in his own country.

10

A CONCLUDING ASSESSMENT

The career of Joseph Chamberlain began a little before Gladstone reached the premiership and ended just before the next great Liberal statesman, Lloyd George, did the same. It was an era in which Britain played a dominant role in the world, and in which the Liberal and Conservative parties controlled political life at home. His personality and achievements place him alongside such renowned figures as Disraeli, Salisbury, Balfour and Asquith, in a period of great political reputations. His death marks the end of that period; on the morning of his passing, he was told the news of the assassination of the Archduke Ferdinand of Sarajevo, the spark which ignited the fire that overwhelmed Europe in 1914.

He had been a key figure in the unfolding development of both Liberal and Conservative parties. Starting as the Nonconformist Radical who mocked the aristocracy and other bastions of privilege, he ended up as the Imperialist whose Unionism and love of Society made him an acceptable guest in many of the leading country houses. Of course, he was not the only distinguished parliamentarian of the 19th and 20th centuries who underwent a political transformation – even Gladstone ended up in a very different position on the political spectrum from where he began. In such a long career, it is perhaps unfair to expect consistency of views, for over such a time situations evolve and people's interests and attitudes change; inevitably, politicians have to react to the situations of the day.

One hundred years ago, it was easier to cross the floor of the House of Commons than it is today, for party boundaries were less rigidly drawn and support could coalesce around an outstanding personality who could create and sway opinion. Furthermore, in any generation, there are some politicians who sit uneasily within the confines of one party. Big personalities can easily find themselves out of step with the grouping of which they are nominally a member; the actions and attitudes of both Lloyd George and Winston Churchill were similarly at variance with the perceived interests of their parties from time to time. Both were prepared to cast aside party labels when they felt the need arose. For Chamberlain, it was the cause for which he worked – at one time, against Home Rule, at another, promoting Tariff Reform – that was more important than consideration of party advantage. He was convinced that he was in the right.

Of course, unlike the other two, Chamberlain never reached the highest office. He was a possible future leader and Prime Minister of either of the two main parties, but he is remembered less for this than as the destructive force whose impact on the Liberals in 1886 and the Tories twenty years later was shattering, throwing both parties into disarray.

He was undoubtedly a divisive figure. He used his influence against Home Rule, so that the Irish were much antagonised by his words and attitudes. The Boers were estranged by the Jameson Raid and his subsequent policy in South Africa. In English politics, he won few friends; despite his cool demeanour, he could arouse fierce opposition in others. His speeches could provoke great bitterness, and his methods could be opportunist, some would say unscrupulous.

Yet this perspective of Chamberlain as a supreme destructive force is no adequate assessment of his contribution to Victorian and Edwardian political life. His career must rank in some sense as a failure, for he never achieved the supreme power for which his abilities and ambitions made him such an obvious candidate – but there was a positive side to his work.

The historian Robert Blake has distinguished between the politicians who wanted to *be* someone, and those like Lloyd George and Chamberlain who wanted to *do* something. Though neither of them was averse to status and acclaim, both can claim to be the architects of particular policies and achievements. In Chamberlain's case, he was, in his early days, the foremost Radical of his generation. It was in his adopted town of Birmingham that he really achieved something permanent.

BIRMINGHAM AND LOCAL GOVERNMENT

Joseph Chamberlain's name is still honoured in Birmingham today, and the spirit of his approach to municipal enterprise lingers on. He wanted to see the town develop into an outstanding example of local administration, for he believed Birmingham society to be 'superior in earnestness, sincerity and natural intelligence to any other'.

His contribution was immense. When he became involved in local government, Birmingham was a relatively backward town compared to many other industrial places which had already begun refashioning their centres. Municipal advance was more associated with Liverpool, Manchester and Glasgow where major improvement schemes were in hand. Chamberlain believed in the importance and dignity of municipal work, and wanted Birmingham to be at the forefront. He and others turned the transformation of their town into a moral crusade. They were prepared to sacrifice their time and energy, and a combination of religious ethics and business sense provided the impulse for the changes which were to be made. As the American observer, Ralph, wrote in 1890;

> Municipal life completely swallowed up commercial life. Birmingham is above all a business city, run by businessmen on business principles.

Chamberlain and his colleagues succeeded in making Birmingham a model of good, efficient town government, and in so doing brought about such a civic renaissance that it became the leading and best governed provincial centre in the country. Chamberlain, with his foresight, dedication and enterprise, was the driving force behind the changes, and it was he who captured the popular imagination. As Asa Briggs has written, he lit 'the fires of zeal in local government', and was able 'to infuse collective vigour into municipal affairs'.

He never forgot the experience of administering a great town, and throughout his life there were echoes of his 'gas-and-water' approach to problems. The Hammonds observed that he later tackled Irish issues in the same straightforward manner, believing that the burning resentments of Irishmen 'could be doused by a bucket of best Birmingham water'. He certainly felt that strong local government on the Birmingham model could transform the Irish situation.

Some people found him too narrow in his outlook. He was always proud to proclaim himself a Birmingham man, and made frequent comparisons citing the town as an example. In 1876, he suggested that local people had had a better deal out of his Improvement Scheme than the nation had out of the purchase of the Suez Canal shares. In the following year, he compared his 'gas-and-water' undertakings with Disraeli's imperial ventures, and, as he said, was so parochially minded that he had greater satisfaction from the civic reform than from the annexation of Cyprus and the Transvaal. What he said of the young Lloyd George might well be said of him; '(He) is a very able man and will go far. It is a pity, however, that he is so provincial in his views'.

The townspeople of Birmingham were justly proud of 'Radical Joe', their hero, and the city became his personal fiefdom. Throughout his career, and those of his sons, Austen and Neville, Birmingham remained loyal to the family tradition. For a long time, its citizens withheld strong backing to the trade unions and early Labour movement because they lived and worked in 'Joe's town'. If he was their man, so Birmingham was his 'home' and it provided him with the platform, Birmingham Town Hall, from which he made most of his pronouncements.

As a politician and successful Midlands industrialist, he was very sensitive to the economic fortunes of the country, with his finger placed firmly on the business pulse. More than any other national politician, he was attuned to the interests of the business community, and he understood and ventilated its grievances.

Britain's industrial supremacy was under threat at the end of the 19th century as it lost the economic benefits of being the first country to industrialise. Its rivals were challenging the long-held lead, and Chamberlain came to see Free Trade, the official Liberal creed, as no longer appropriate. He looked for opportunities within the Empire, and his solution, a programme of Imperial Preference, was open to question. Yet to a greater degree than most politicians, he understood the condition of Britain's manufacturing base, and that the prosperity of Birmingham and the Black Country was as essential part of it. The ebbing fortunes of the city and its surrounding region played a significant role in helping him to work out his theory and policy for the Empire.

Overall, Birmingham had a profound influence on him and he on it, and he is remembered as the man who dreamed a great dream, and whose vision has continued to inspire many of the decision-makers of the 20th century. For local people, he is still regarded as the 'Father of Modern Birmingham'.

A MODERN PROFESSIONAL POLITICIAN
—

His contribution as a civic leader and his continuing commitment to the borough's fortunes are part of his more creative legacy, but he is also remembered for his skill as a professional politician, in particular as a platform orator and an astute party organiser. The British system of parliamentary democracy is based upon political parties, and he saw the challenge which the 1867 Reform Act had presented to them. A new age had dawned in British political life, and he was keen that the Liberals should seize their opportunity.

Again, Birmingham provided the inspiration. An organisation was needed to attract the newly enfranchised voters, and the creation of a Liberal caucus can be attributed to a number of people of drive and ability, such as William Harris and Francis Schnadhorst. Chamberlain was a key figure who deployed his considerable organisational gifts in tackling the 'two votes, three members clause'. He also appreciated that:

> The working classes who cannot contribute pecuniarily though they are often ready to sacrifice a more than proportionate amount of time and labour, are now the majority in most borough constituencies, and no candidate and no policy has a chance of success unless their goodwill and active support can first be secured.

While critics saw the caucus as an instrument of tyranny, to him its aim was

> essentially democratic. It is to provide for the full and efficient representation of the will of the majority and for its definite expression in the government of the people.

Others felt that under the guise of democracy, power was concentrated in the hands of a faction, and that small group was dominated by the dictatorial figure of Chamberlain who in influence, if not in stature, towered over his colleagues. A contemporary cartoon showed him addressing a New Street crowd, with the words 'Now lads, let's be equal and I will be your King'.

Yet the people of Birmingham were always much involved in the political life of the town. They volunteered to help the Liberal cause in great numbers, and massive enthusiasm was generated, so that public meetings were large and lively. As well as helping to mould opinion, the caucus also expressed public feeling and enthusiasm.

Standing for the electorate against the old order, for the people's will against oligarchy, Chamberlain realised that democracy was on the march. He was ready to put himself at its head with a programme radical in content, and demagogic in its form of presentation.

The influence of the Birmingham Liberal Federation was considerable. Copied elsewhere, it was also the model for the National Liberal Federation which for several years maintained its headquarters in Birmingham. Many Liberals, particularly the Whigs, became alarmed by the power of this extra-parliamentary organisation, particularly given the control which Chamberlain was seen to wield over it.

Yet when he deserted the Liberal cause and the NLF transferred its loyalty to Gladstone, Birmingham continued to offer solid backing to Chamberlain. His skills in the field of party organisation were such that he could retain his Birmingham base for the Unionist cause. With a clearly defined policy of Tariff Reform, he held the loyalty of his supporters locally and then set out to capture the National Union of Conservative Associations for his new cause.

As a public speaker in Parliament or on the stage at the Town Hall, he had few equals. His style was hard-hitting and robust, appealing to popular passions and prejudices. Throughout his life, he could inspire his Birmingham supporters to peaks of enthusiasm and arouse in his opponents feelings of outrage and venom. From being somewhat formal and stilted in his early debating days, he became supremely accomplished. Never dull, his razor wit and clear voice made him easy on the ear; his voice also carried so well that he could always be heard in every part of the building.

The Speaker of the House of Commons is perhaps in the best position to judge parliamentary performance, seeing and hearing countless politicians of every sort. Speaker Peel, who heard some excellent performers, believed that Chamberlain was 'the best speaker in the House with one exception, and the best debater without exception'.

For all the enthusiasm he could arouse, on many occasions he actually spoke with restraint and self-mastery, so that Margot Asquith could conclude that his 'opponents were snowed under by his accumulated moderation'. Winston Churchill, however, has perhaps left us with the most vivid picture of Chamberlain's hold over an audience. In 1900, Churchill invited Chamberlain to speak on his behalf at Oldham. In *My Early Life*, he subsequently wrote;

> There was more enthusiasm over him at this moment than after the Great War for Mr Lloyd George and Sir Douglas Haig combined. There was at the same time a tremendous opposition; but antagonism had not wholly excluded admiration from their

breast . . . I watched my honoured guest with close attention. He loved the roar of the multitude, and with my father could always say, 'I have never feared the English democracy'. The blood mantled in his cheek, and his eye, as it caught mine, twinkled with pure enjoyment . . . Inside the meeting, we were all surprised at Mr Chamberlain's restraint. His soft purring voice and reasoned incisive sentences, for most of which he had a careful note, made a remarkable impression. He spoke for over an hour, but what pleased the audience most was that, having made a mistake in some fact or figure to the prejudice of his opponents, he went back and corrected it, observing that he must not be unfair'.

ACHIEVEMENTS IN NATIONAL POLITICS
—

When it comes to his actual achievements in national politics, the record is disappointing, for Chamberlain was hamstrung in the administrations in which he held office by the fact that his views were not held by the majority of the Cabinet. Particularly between 1880-85, his speeches and actions were perhaps ill-calculated to win much support from colleagues to whom he was often an embarrassment. Later, under Salisbury, his reforming scope was limited, and as his Radical zeal was waning, he became more interested in the affairs of the Empire.

Back in 1880, he had spoken of his desire to secure for the nation the same social improvements he had brought to the people of Birmingham, for otherwise it would have been a sadness to have 'given up the Town Council for the Cabinet'.

Yet as a Minister, he was frustrated by the limitations of office, and the Irish issue effectively preoccupied the politics of the 1880s so that Gladstone had a reason or an excuse for not tackling social questions with any urgency. In these days, though he could champion parliamentary reform and speak persuasively for the Radical cause, Chamberlain never had the power and influence to see his mission accomplished.

His scope was similarly limited as a Conservative and Unionist, and, anyway, by the time he was in the Salisbury Cabinet, his desire for far-reaching change had given way to a new enthusiasm, the cause of Empire. He was perhaps a surprising person to lead the Imperial cause, representing as he did such an inland city. However, as noted, Birmingham's dependence on commerce made its fluctuating fortunes in the Great Depression of the 1880s very relevant to his outlook towards the Empire and, later, Tariff Reform.

On the political right, he is remembered primarily as an Imperialist statesman, for the Empire and its associated fiscal plans absorbed his attention as a minister and backbencher. His dream of welding the areas of the Empire under one 'Supreme and Imperial Parliament', and the close links he favoured in defence and commerce, never materialised. However, his views caught the mood of late-Victorian Imperialism as an expression of British patriotic feeling. Furthermore, his reforming work at the Colonial Office was worthwhile and of lasting significance, even if inadequate funds were made available for him to carry out all his proposals. Similarly, his policy of encouraging the federal movement in Australia was successful in cementing friendship within the Empire, and in securing the loyal support of the Australian government and people when it was needed in the Boer War.

His interest in Imperialism was largely inspired by a conviction that there were opportunities for manufacturers and their employees within the Empire. This search for economic advantage is a theme running through his policies towards the African continent as well as the older colonies of Canada, Australia and New Zealand. Tariff Reform was designed to assist British businessmen as they strove to compete with foreign manufacturers, and to provide work for those who currently lacked it.

The fiasco of the Jameson Raid has given his opponents an opportunity to portray him as an Imperialist adventurer. The early setbacks and the methods later employed to win the Boer War did much to damage the Imperial dream. The war fought on behalf of that vision ended by discrediting the whole idea in the eyes of many people.

What had become apparent was that policies of Imperialism always required a national army to support them. Chamberlain had once categorised colonial policy in this way;

> We are to keep what belongs to us. We are to peg out our claims
> for posterity. If anyone tries to rush these claims, we are to stop
> them.

To stop them would, of course, involve the use of armed strength and for anti-Imperialists this was the crux of the case. Such critics were and are unlikely to find the performance of the later Chamberlain to their liking.

As for Tariff Reform, this was a crusade he happily took up to provide a new cause for the exhausted Balfour Government. He saw it as highly desirable to bring about 'the maintenance and increase of the national strength, and the prosperity of the United Kingdom'. Beyond this, as he remarked in October 1903:

> the object is, or should be, the realisation of the greatest ideal which has ever inspired statesmen in any country or in any age – the creation of an Empire such as the world has ever seen.

He was unsuccessful in his efforts, for ultimately he was unable to convince the British people or indeed his party that such beneficial results could follow. His vigorous pursuit of his beliefs was at least a contributory factor in the restoration of Liberal unity and the defeat of the Unionists in 1906, which put them out of office for the rest of his life.

In fact, in national politics, he is remembered more by many people for his resignations than for his achievements. Like any politician, on occasion he was inevitably faced with difficult choices over how best to exert his influence – whether to remain a member of the Cabinet and fight from the inside, or whether to go to the backbenches and lead a more direct attack.

In 1886 and 1903, he resigned. In the first case, over Home Rule, there must be some doubt about the wisdom of his decision. He was prepared to go so far along the road to devolved government that it is questionable whether the difference in principle between him and Gladstone was worth the struggle. The likelihood is that Home Rule would have been defeated in the House of Lords anyway, with far less cost to Chamberlain's reputation. He would have been in a good position to pick up the pieces after such a Liberal setback, as an alternative leader who had never been committed to Home Rule.

In that case, however, he could hardly avoid making a judgement, for when Gladstone underwent his conversion, others had to decide on their response. In 1903, he was in no such position; there was no necessity to take up the divisive issue of Tariff Reform. The differences between him and Balfour were not fundamental, being more concerned with party tactics than the substance of policy. By leaving the Government, he sacrificed his power base, and pinned all his hopes on a popular campaign taken to the country. He underestimated the opposition which his policy would arouse as he tried to foist it on both the party and the public.

On both occasions, he may have done better to use his leverage within the Cabinet, with the chance of persuading others to adopt his viewpoint. He could claim to represent widely held opinions, and over Tariff Reform he had the tacit backing of a sympathetic leader. He might also have used his Cabinet position more effectively in March 1903 over the Budget. He was unfortunate to be out of the country at the key time, just as he was unlucky to be out of action when the party leadership fell vacant on Salisbury's retirement.

HIS PLACE ON THE PARTY SPECTRUM

Overall, in his career, two divisive issues stand out, Home Rule and Tariff Reform. His actions on these had a devastating effect on the parties with which he was aligned. He split the Liberals and pitched them out of office, and then, twenty years later, wrecked the chances of the Conservatives. When controversial issues arose, it was clear party was not his first loyalty.

He had been a Radical, he became a Unionist, but he was never a socialist. Sometimes it is argued that if he had not found it necessary to abandon the Gladstonians in 1886 and had, in due course, succeeded to the leadership, he could have given the Liberals a new direction. A distinct Labour Party would have been rendered unnecessary if the Liberals had more effectively embraced his Radical ideas of social improvement, as there would have been little more room on the left wing of politics.

This is very unlikely. He was a Radical whose rhetoric was always more extreme than the objectives he was pursuing. As a businessman, he was interested in efficiency in government and administration, and in the direct practical improvement in the lives of working men. His proposals were meant to be an antidote to the socialism of which he strongly disapproved. Like Balfour, he could distinguish between social and socialist legislation, and of the latter he was a direct opponent.

As a Radical, he abhorred all manifestations of privilege, but he had no wish to take up socialist policies of wholesale redistribution of wealth and public ownership of industry. He approved of self-reliance and free enterprise, and wanted to make the existing system work more efficiently and justly. He was prepared to use municipal and state power to resolve particular problems, and as a pragmatist could see good reasons for the local authorities to run water or gas services. Indeed, in the 1880s, he could say that he was 'enough of a socialist to believe that services which by their nature best function as monopolies should be under public control', whether this was by outright ownership or by regulation.

However, it is noteworthy that the building improvements he planned were not undertaken directly by the local authorities – rather, the council regulated the private contractors involved. With housing policy, also, there was no positive promotion of a policy of constructing homes for the working classes in reclaimed inner city areas; the initiative was again left to speculative builders in the suburbs.

While he possessed a general belief that the existing distribution of wealth was too unequal, this was far short of a commitment to socialism, which he associated with class warfare. Unlike Manchester, Birmingham had not been noted for its class divisions, and there was not such a wide gulf between the artisan and the business owner. In the small workshop economy of the Black Country, it was easy for him to convince himself that there was an identity of interests between workers and capitalists. As a modern 'one-nation' Conservative, Peter Walker, MP has written;

> [His creed would have avoided] the dangers of class conflict in the Conservatism of the market economy. Chamberlain's policy was one of class harmony, both worker and capitalist alike are held to have a stake in Britain's prosperity.

A LOST LEADER AND PRIME MINISTER

He was a dynamic force, a coming man in politics whose career held great promise. Yet he never reached the prize he sought, that of party leadership. This was not from want of ambition, nor because of lack of ability. For some, the fault lay in his background. Thus Lord Esher could write:

> Chamberlain's faults all come from his upbringing. Clever as he is, he has never learnt the self-restraint which everybody learns at a great public school or at university.

To such members of the aristocracy, he was always likely to be socially unacceptable, and this coloured their judgement of his contribution. As a self-made businessman, Chamberlain was not prepared to follow convention and take the accepted route to the top. Upper-class politicians could never see him as a gentleman and were, like Queen Victoria, shocked by both his aggressive manner and the inflammatory language of many of his speeches.

In the end, neither Liberals nor Conservatives felt at ease with him. He created enemies by his implacable and cold personality, and had difficulty in dealing with people whose attitudes were hostile to his; he could not win them round to his viewpoint.